THE GHANA REVOLUTION
From Nkrumah to Jerry Rawlings

By

Ebenezer Babatope

Fourth Dimension Publishing Co., Ltd.

First Published 1982 by
FOURTH DIMENSION PUBLISHING CO., LTD
16 Fifth Avenue, City Layout. PMB. 01164, Enugu, Nigeria.
Tel+234-42-459969. Fax+234-42-456904.
email: fdpbooks@aol.com, fdpbooks@yahoo.com
Web site: http://www.fdpbooks.com.

Reprinted 2002

© Ebenezer Babatope 1982

ISBN 978-156-210-2

CONDITIONS OF SALE

All rights reserved. No part of this publication may be reproduced, stored in a retrieval system, or transmitted in any form or by any means, electronic, mechanical, photocopying, recording, or otherwise without the prior permission of the publisher.

Photoset and printed in Nigeria by
Fourth Dimension Publishers, Enugu.

DEDICATION

Dedicated to Kwame Nkrumah, the torchbearer of African freedom, who spent his entire life fighting for the liberation of Africa. He tried his best as a lone ranger in his own time. His efforts were sabotaged by imperialism but Nkrumah lives forever in the hearts of all African patriots who have drawn inspiration from his life.

CONTENTS

Foreword ix
Introduction xiii

Chapter
1 Nkrumah and Nkrumaism 1
2 Busia and Acheampong 11
3 The Collapse of Acheampong's "Revolution" 23
4 The Tragedy of Akuffo 39
5 The Collapse of the Third Republic 51
6 The Jerry Rawlings Factor 57
7 Corruption in High Places 67
8 Proclamation of the Ghana Revolution 73
9 Dialogue with the Revolutionaries 81
10 The Ghana Revolution — An Evaluation 93
11 The Ghana Revolution Must Succeed 103
   Index 106

Foreword

The presence of Kwame Nkrumah is again being felt in Ghana. After more than fifteen years of reaction against everything the man advocated and strove for, Ghana has recognised with hindsight the vision of a united, self-reliant, socialist Africa that drove Nkrumah to commit the resources and future of the country in a deadly confrontation with imperialist powers. The nations of Africa owe much to Nkrumah and his comrades, Frantz Fanon, Patrice Lumuba, Gamal Nasser who sought an independence beyond the formal declaration intended by the colonialist powers to appease the shallow personal ambitions of their black stooges. That these men perished in the struggle by no means closes the chapter on their role in the African Revolution, as Nkrumah so aptly labelled the ongoing struggle for economic, as well as political independence of the African continent.

Professor Busia spent the energies of his administration suppressing the demand for Nkrumah's return and the return of anything identified with the proscribed CPP. Afrifa, Acheampong, Akuffo and their military comrades paid with their lives for their reactionary encouragement of neo-colonial interests and suppression of the African Revolution and the immediate needs of the impoverished masses. Yet the legacy of Nkrumah lives on and has resurfaced, according to the author of this book and my good friend, Ebenezer Babatope, in a most improbable form — a military administration — which took power on 31st December 1981, following the coup led by Jerry Rawlings recently retired from the Ghanaian Air force by the same civilian administration brought to power and removed by him.

Is Nkrumah to be blamed for Ghana's chequered history following his demise? So much has been written on the man and his ideas; nearly all of it biased one way or the other. The dynamic, charismatic character of the man intimidated and frustrated his enemies and blindfolded his ardent supporters. Only a few have been able to look objectively at the man and assess his contribution to the liberation of Africa and the Third World peoples. Mokwugo Okoye has stated succinctly what history is confirming about the legacy of Nkrumah:

> The historical importance of Kwame Nkrumah is that, more than anyone else, he quickened the pace of liberation in Africa (and) inflamed revolution in many parts that never knew it. When he was in power, he followed a dynamic African policy designed to achieve the unity of the continent and rid it of all the vestiges of colonialism and racism ... Nkrumah established the African presence in the world community and restored the dignity of the blackman which he made a burning issue in all international tribunuals. ("Nkrumah and the African Dream", *Embattled Men,* p.203).

Ebenezer Babatope has created yet another very readable book which states in a consistent manner the ideals for which he stands. He has spent considerable time in Ghana and has followed the political life of that country with much interest. He has talked with those actively engaged in the "Ghana Revolution" and has added his own perspective to their views. He believes strongly that Ghana is emerging once again, though bankrupt and disheartened, as a revolutionary state in the hands of Jerry Rawlings.

The Ghana Revolution was proclaimed by Rawlings on 8th

January 1982. "Nkrumaism" has been encouraged by the Rawlings' administration, but as Ebenezer Babatope points out, Rawlings has not yet taken the necessary administrative steps nor defined sufficiently the ideological base of the Revolution to attract the masses' support. The Ghanaian Revolution, like the larger African Revolution, exists only on paper and in the mouths of a few dedicated persons, lacking two essential factors for any revolution: an astute and seasoned leadership and the support and creative energies of the masses.

Jerry Rawlings believes in the Revolution he is pursuing; whether or not he will be able to translate that belief into action will be the real test of his administration. The people of Ghana are ready for a change and will support any person or policy that will bring them employment and food. No revolution can survive in the midst of mass physical and psychological pain without engendering a violent reactionary reversal of the ideological framework of the revolution and the rise of reactionary elements within the social structure. Jerry Rawlings has a heavy task before him to restore the economy of the country and the positive mentality of the people. He has taken a necessary step in seeking Nigeria's goodwill, even though ideologies differ.

I share Ebenezer Babatope's hope in the Ghana Revolution and I watch for signs that it is indeed taking hold. Nigeria has failed to take up the leadership position left vacant by Ghana. The OAU has failed in Chad; it has been ineffectual in its stand against apartheid. The African continent as a whole lacks the leadership needed to achieve the necessary unity of purpose to propound and enforce policies that would result in an "African presence" in international relations. A dangerous vacuum has developed, resulting in internal squabbles among nations of the OAU, supposedly united by a common purpose, and contradictory, embarrassing national stands against fundamental policies of that body.

Because of her leadership potential, Nigeria must shoulder the blame for the present state of African affairs. Her return to civilian rule has failed to activate her own economy and establish her weight in international politics, let alone find means of galvanising her neighbours into progressive and productive action. As this administration draws to a close, it is imperative that we challenge all contenders in the 1983 elections to reassess their national policies in the light of the larger whole. As Nigeria struggles to survive the effects of her unwillingness to establish a self-reliant economy, she should take stock of the causes of her economic failure. I believe with Nkrumah that even if we succeed in salvaging our economy from the grip of multinational conglomerates and from dependence on the exploitation of a single non-productive resource, we must keep in mind that our economic independence is but a means to the total liberation, unification and social transformation of Africa.

The nations of Africa have tolerated a situation in which economic, defense and communications links with outside powers have reduced them to mere stooges on the world scene. Nigeria should take the lead in transferring the power structure from outside to within the continent. If she does not assume that responsibility, her day, like Ghana's, will pass, and the African continent will remain in the stranglehold of imperialist powers.

It is pertinent to note in closing that Kwame Nkrumah's two books — *Neo-Colonialism, The Last Stage of Imperialism* (which first exposed the exploitation of African multinationals) and *Consciencism* (which advocates the synthesis of the Euro-christian and the Islamic cultures as an ideology for the economic development of Africa) — were, and still are, the most authentic ideological framework for African integration. They are part of the legacy that the great Nkrumah has left behind.

Ebenezer Babatope sees the Ghana Revolution as an embodiment of Nkrumaism. Perhaps this nostalgia is the beginning of a reawakening on the continent to the ideals of those who fought imperialism in its most drastic form — colonialism. If so, the world will surely experience an African Revolution that will change the face of the world economic and political structure.

Arthur A. Nwankwo

Introduction

"I have never regarded the struggle for the independence of the Gold Coast as an isolated objective but always as a part of a general world historical pattern. The African in every territory of this vast continent has been awakened and the struggle for freedom will go on. It is our duty as the vanguard force to offer what assistance we can to those now engaged in the battles that we ourselves have fought and won. Our task is not done and our own safety is not assured until the last vestiges of colonialism have been swept from Africa." That was "OSAGYEFO" Kwame Nkrumah in the conclusion of his autobiography *Ghana the Autobiography of Kwame Nkrumah*.

There is no way one can talk of the African revolution without mentioning the name of Kwame Nkrumah. It was he who ignited the patriotism of many Africans and inspired them to fight for the political and economic freedom of Africa. Nkrumah was a lone ranger in this crusade, a factor that contributed immensely to the ease with which imperialism was able to subvert his regime and plan his eventual overthrow.

On 24th February 1966, Kwame Nkrumah was overthrown by a section of the Ghana Army led by the late General Emmanuel Kotoka and the late General Amansa Akwasi Afrika (then a major). The coup terminated a regime that had offered great hope for the African people and halted the rapid advance of Ghana to modernity. Ghanaian soldiers paraded around the streets of Accra, hailing the fall of immortal Kwame Nkrumah and pulling down his statue. All his works were destroyed and an attempt made to completely wipe out his memory from the minds of the Ghanaian people.

However it is impossible to halt the forward march of history. No one has ever succeeded in ultimately stemming the course of revolution and change. Nkrumah represented a political passion, enthusiasm and dynamism that will continue to live. The flames are now burning across the entire continent, posing very serious problems to the antics and machinations of world imperialism.

The overthrow of Kwame Nkrumah initiated the political and economic decline of the great country Nkrumah had envisioned. Today, Ghana is a shadow of its former self. Ghana, the tiny Ghana, that once dictated the pace of Africa's revolutionary strides to freedom, has been turned into a country with no soul, no principles and no direction. Ghana since 1966 has been piloted aimlessly by purposeless leaders who are mere pawns in the hands of world imperialist forces.

During his exile in Conakry, Guinea, Nkrumah fought doggedly to re-establish a progressive Ghana. He published many books on the African revolution to fire the resolve of his countrymen to re-establish for themselves a glorious and dignified history. He made patriotic broadcasts to the Ghana people to rise against lackeys of imperialism in military uniform. He addressed rallies and in 1970 when the Portuguese fascist invasion of Guinea was launched, Nkrumah fought alongside his fellow African revolutionary, Sekou Toure. The people of Ghana then living under illusions refused to listen to the old man. But Nkrumah's books, ideas and thoughts contributed in no small measure to the building up of a new generation of Africans who are prepared to continue with the prosecution of the African Revolution where Nkrumah stopped.

Today, we are all witnesses of the freedom of Angola, Mozambique and Zimbabwe. Very soon, Namibia will join the committee of free nations of Africa. Nkrumah died in Bucharest, Rumania on the 27th April 1972 but, with the flames of independence and freedom which he ignited still burning on in Africa, the ideals for which he stood will live forever.

On 8th January 1982, the Ghana Revolution was proclaimed by Jerry Rawlings in a workers' rally in Accra. The following report was despatched by the Reuter News Agency on the historic event:

> Flight Lieutenant Jerry Rawlings, Head of Ghana's ruling provisional national defence council which seized power in a coup last week, has urged his countrymen to carry out a revolution. From an armoured car, he told thousands of cheering workers at a rally in central Accra on Friday, January 8, 1982 to "take the initiative of revolution into your hands". He told the rally that the revolution had to cut across the lines between the military, police and civilians. The crowds waved placards and chanted "The holy war means hard work" and "J. J. the saviour" — a reference to the leader's first names, Jerry John.
>
> They had arrived at the Black Star Square in buses, trucks, cars and on foot after demonstrating through the streets of the capital in support of their new military rulers.

This book deals in the main with the Ghanaian revolution officially declared by Jerry John Rawlings in Ghana after the 31st December 1981 coup that ousted the regime of Hilla Limann. The coming of Jerry Rawlings into Ghana politics since 1979 signals the return of the Ghana Kwame Nkrumah had envisioned. All the forces of reaction are now being silenced by Jerry John Rawlings. Ghana has been reborn and the Nkrumaist teachings of old have again found their way back to an African country that was once the Mecca of the glorious African revolution.

I have tried to examine the political events in Ghana since 1966 and I have equally tried in this small book to show that a people's freedom can never be denied no matter the forces of coercion and intimidation that may be unleashed against them. The Ghanaian people who have been under political enslavement since 1966 have now broken the chains of oppression by the coming of Jerry John Rawlings. The younger generation of Ghanaians who are now the guiding spirit of the Ghana revolution are poised for a decisive fight against all the reactionary forces that had sentenced the lives of millions of Ghanaian citizens to misery, ignorance, frustration and despair.

There are, however, problems in the new Ghana of Jerry Rawlings which, if care is not taken, may disrupt the revolution and consequently halt its advance. I have tried to examine some of these in this small book and I have offered my suggestions in the belief that the young revolutionary forces in Ghana will try to study and consider them. It is important for all African revolutionaries and patriots to protect the Ghanaian Revolution. It is the task of all socialist forces to ensure a lasting victory for the Ghanaian people. When Nkrumah declared in 1957 on the occasion of Ghana's independence that the independence of Ghana would be meaningless unless linked with the total independence of Africa, he was of course speaking the obvious. Ghana's independence and her commitment to continental freedom under the watchful eyes of Kwame Nkrumah opened the gates for the independence of many African countries.

The Ghanaian revolution, directed by Jerry Rawlings and the men of the Provisional National Defence Council (P.N.D.C.), will certainly determine the future course of events in Africa. The success of the revolution in Ghana will surely lead to more revolutions in Africa in the light of the many repressive and reactionary fascist regimes springing up every day in Africa.

Imperialism encourages the growth of fascist regimes in many countries of the world to subvert progressive governments. Fascist regimes are built up on the alliance of the elite core in industry, banking, universities, police, judiciary and the military. The essence of fascism is to protect capitalism and its dangerous interests. Fascism also subverts national liberation efforts as its ruthless apparatus is spread to stem the growing tide of nationalism in many countries.

The Ghanaian revolution must therefore be jealously protected. The revolutionaries must also ensure that their revolution does not degenerate, paving the way clear for the emergence of a fascist regime in Ghana. If Ghana fails, then African revolutionaries and socialist militants are doomed. May it not happen.

Jerry Rawlings must not surrender to imperialism nor capitulate to reactionary forces. He must adopt correct ideological methods to guide the Ghanaian revolution and he must learn from the mistakes of Nkrumah and fashion a new Nkrumaist approach to consolidating and advancing Ghana's independence for Kwame Nkrumah is to Ghana what Jose Marti was to Cuba, Sun-Yat-Sen to China, Kemal Atartürk to Turkey and Vladimir Ilyich Lenin to the Soviet Union.

This is no scholarly research work. Neither does the author lay claim to any intellectual contribution. It is an honest contribution of a progressive Nigerian freelance journalist and politician to the successful prosecution of the glorious African revolution. I accept whatever might be the errors, faults and omissions of this book. I do believe all readers of this book will take the book as they find it.

Victory certainly will go to all oppressed people who live by their toil, labour and meagre resources to sustain the rule of wicked exploiters of our land. The days of the economic armed robbers of our continent are numbered; one day will produce everlasting victory and triumph for the wretched of the earth. Jerry Rawling's experiment in Ghana is a full testimony and confirmation of this inevitable situation.

Long live the Ghana Revolution. Long live Nkrumaism. Long live the AFRICAN REVOLUTION.

Ebenezer Babatope
LAGOS
July 1982

1
Nkrumah and Nkrumaism

The Ghanaian revolution proclaimed by Jerry John Rawlings can not be discussed objectively without a brief revisit of the life and times of Kwame Nkrumah. Nkrumaism which was described as a useless philosophy by the misled section of the Ghana Army which overthrew the government on the 24th February 1966 has now become a potent weapon in the hands of the young Ghanaian revolutionaries. Nkrumaism, with the coming of Jerry John Rawlings, is once again on the upsurge.

It is pertinent to ask at this stage, what is Nkrumaism?

Nkrumaism is the philosophy of the African Revolution. It has a clear and unambiguous socialist character. This feature is clearly reflected in Kwame Nkrumah's book *Class Struggle in Africa*. Kwame Nkrumah knew that for an ideology to grip the masses there must be emphasis placed on education. It was for this reason that he established the famous "Ideological Institute" at Winneba — a symbol of people's education. The school was one of the socialist citadels destroyed by the imperialist conspirators on 24th February 1966.

Kwame Nkrumah advocated very seriously a revolution for the African people, a revolution that will no doubt be protracted but that will finally bring victory for all the people of Africa. The African Revolution as defined by Nkrumaism is deeply rooted in the waging of a relentless struggle against imperialism, colonialism and neo-colonialism. The African Revolution also aims at combating effectively the activities of agents, lackeys and errand boys of the aforementioned evils.

The African Revolution propounded by Kwame Nkrumah includes the consolidation of the independence of all African countries. This consolidation demands the following: (1) waging continuous wars with world imperialist forces until all their traces have been erased and destroyed from all parts of the continent. The independence of Angola, Mozambique and Zimbabwe has already justified this noble principle. The struggle for the total liberation of the rest of Africa still under imperialist domination, however, continues (eye witness accounts of events in free Angola and Zimbabwe form an appendix to this book).

(2) The application of the severest punishment to all imperialists and their known native allies who may try at any time to overthrow the progressive governments of the people.

(3) The need for African leaders to be ideological so that they can be adequately prepared even at the risk of their lives to launch their countries on paths that lead to progress and to the eradication of all forms of exploitation, intimidation, oppression, suppression and inhumanity of man against man.

(4) The African Revolution also supports the just struggles of the peoples of Africa who are fighting to shake off the yoke of colonialism.

Nkrumaism springs from a socialist ideology that gives clear expression to Marxist principles within the context of present day conditions in Africa. Lenin justified this when he declared unequivocally that each state would eventually achieve its own revolution.

Kwame Nkrumah as part of his planned education of the masses established a great press that served as the mouthpiece of genuine revolutionaries the world over. The progressive press produced the *Spark* magazine, a magazine that thundered the rhythm of the great African Revolution and made the imperialists and all enemies of Africa tremble that their time was at an end on our continent.

The editors of *Spark* were dedicated African patriots who were all assembled in Ghana as the country became the leader of the African struggles for true and total continental unity. These editors once wrote the following as part of the definition of Nkrumaism:

> Nkrumah rejects outright the notion that the aim of imperialism is to bring civilisation to a people (doctrine of assimilation) or to prepare them for self-rule (doctrine of trusteeship). Imperialism, he asserts, is a doctrine of exploitation. In terms of government it is the policy which aims at creating, organising and maintaining an Empire. Contemporary imperialism is the dominance of industrial capital which was preceded historically by the dominance of merchant capital.

In the *Accra Evening News* of 14th January 1949, Nkrumah analysed the case of Nkrumaism as follows: "The strength of the organised masses is invisible. We must organise as never before, for organisation decides everything."

In his book *Africa Must Unite* Nkrumah came out clearly in the special advice he gave to members of any nationalist movement. This advice he gave in the form of a Chinese poem:

> Go to the people
> Live among them
> Learn from them
> Love them
> Serve them

Plan with them
Start with what they know
Build on what they have

That formed the base of Nkrumaism. Nkrumah was for the people's interests; hence Nkrumaism is bound to become the revolutionary catechism of the new revolutionaries in Ghana who are poised to revive and improve the glorious days of old.

Essential features of Nkrumaism also include:

(1) An undivided Ghana — united in true independence

(2) One united and indivisible continent of Africa. This he said can only be achieved through a continental union government.

(3) Large-scale socio-economic reforms to eliminate and eradicate all colonial institutions.

(4) The struggle for economic independence of African states based on socialist principles.

(5) Establishment of an African High Command to combat all imperialist and racist forces in Africa.

(6) the radical restructuring of the neo-colonial economy most African countries in such a way that socialism is enthroned. Nkrumaism advocates a socialist democracy that will give the people control over the means of production and distribution.

Nkrumaism was making steady progress in Ghana before the imperialist conspiracy of 24th February 1966 terminated its advance. A National Liberation Council was established after the 1966 coup with Lt. General Ankrah as its chairman. Lt.-General Ankrah was, however, humiliated out of power upon the discovery that he was more interested in promoting a personal power regime than in the overall welfare of the people of Ghana. A once revolutionary Ghana under Nkrumah became a major centre of reaction. Jerry Rawlings and the young Turks in Ghana are now attempting to create a new Ghana society based on the teachings of Nkrumaism.

The June 4th movement in Ghana of 1979, which could have cemented Nkrumaism once more in Ghana, missed its goal as most of the leaders of the movement within the Armed forces were not ideological. Jerry Rawlings himself has recently admitted his naivety in the affair that saw the end of some military rulers in Ghana.

That date could have heralded the re-entry of Nkrumaism into Ghana, but for the apparent disinterestedness of the Armed Forces Revolutionary Council, which frustrated such a laudable and patriotic goal.

The 31st December 1981 coup however proclaimed once more the dawn of the glorious African revolution. The coup threw into public limelight all the democratic forces that had for years laboured for a rediscovery of the greatness of Ghana of old. However, the resurgence of Nkrumaism was not done without opposition from the reactionary forces in Ghana. It was a costly exercise that took a heavy toll on human life. A brief sketch of the historical events that set the stage for the revolution following the overthrow of Nkrumah reveals the ideological bankruptcy of the leadership.

For three and a half years following Nkrumah's overthrow, members of the National Liberation Council (NLC), aided in their nefarious activities by imperialists and neo-colonialists, turned the hands of the clock back in the progress made in Ghana under Nkrumah and suppressed the democratic freedoms of the people. Then, in August 1969, these military liars cleverly paved the way for the emergence of late Professor Kofi Abrefa Busia.

Busia, the man the military junta brought to replace the never say die Kwame, was to become a believer in "dialogue" with Vorster's South Africa. With the emergence of Busia, Ghana, formerly the centre of Pan Africanism, became the capital of neo-colonialism. All Africans who were not citizens of Ghana were ordered out of the country. The citizens of Ghana whose fundamental rights had been suppressed for a long time, began to voice their disagreement with the Busia-led neo-colonial government. The unpopularity of the Busia government grew until Busia and his ministers became objects of public ridicule and they were hooted, insulted and jeered at on the streets of Ghana.

By 1970, the people of Ghana had started to make open demands for the return of Nkrumaism. The students were first to set the ball rolling when the National Union of Ghana Students demanded the recall of Kwame Nkrumah. In August 1971, the People's Popular Party, led by a Marxist-Nkrumaist lawyer, John Hansen (he now serves as the P.N.D.C. secretary for interior), sold two thousand photographs of Nkrumah at a mass rally in Kumasi. Henceforth, a wave of terrorism was unleashed on the people of Ghana by the Busia government. Student leaders were brought to parliament to apologise to a group of renegade politicians.

In September 1971, a member of the opposition condemned the Busia policy of dismantling state firms and handing over these state industries to private enterprise, confirming the demand for a return to the socialist programmes of Nkrumah.

In October 1971, amid growing tension for the return of Kwame Nkrumah, the Busia government issued a bill through Parliament under a bogus and fascist designed certificate of urgency for the purpose of outlawing all the demands for Nkrumah and the big ideological weapon "Nkrumaism".

The Law, passed in a most undemocratic manner, amended the Criminal Code and made it a criminal offence for anybody to advocate for the return of Kwame Nkrumah or for the restoration of Nkrumaism. The law prohibited the display of any banner, bunting, ensign, flag, colours, symbol or other insignia of the great Convention People's Party, the singing or playing of any songs associated with the C.P.P. and the use of any slogan by word or by writing which were formerly used by the C.P.P. These offences were made punishable with a prison sentence of five years.

Busia's unrealistic ambitions caused him to attack the Ghana Trade Union Congress which in the days of Nkrumah had been a potent force for the defence of the African Revolution. The complete redeployment of versatile trade union leaders in Ghana as ambassadors rendered defenceless the socialist programmes of Nkrumah. The unfortunate situation left the militarists with easy penetration of Nkrumah's Ghana. Busia knowing fully well the radical force of the Ghana Trade Union Congress made laws that totally incapacitated the union and rendered the union's leaders powerless. In the middle of September 1971, under the same certification of urgency, an Act was passed, after "several hours of debate." according to the *Ghanaian Times*, dissolving the Trade Union Congress. Its bank accounts were frozen and the Congress was taken over by the Progress Party.

On the 13th January 1972, the contradictions that had been planted in Ghana since 1966 exploded and swept off from power those who had been the perpetrators of imperialism. Colonel Ignatius Kutu Acheampong staged a dawn coup and announced the dismissal of the Busia government while the latter was away in Britain for medical treatment. Kofi Abrefa Busa died later in exile.

Unfortunately, subsequent rulers in Ghana after the Busia era merely gambled and toyed with power, instituting no meaningful programmes for the people's welfare. The 4th June military coup of 1979 led by Jerry John Rawlings and the Armed Forces Revolutionary Council was an attempt to reconstruct the entire socio-political history of Ghana. The 4th June 1979 affair, despite its ideological bankruptcy, paved the way for the proclamation of the Ghana Revolution by Jerry John Rawlings on 31st December, 1981.

The road to the Ghana Revolution has indeed been thorny, the problems that ignited the Revolution were multifarious. The reactionary forces inside and outside of Ghana prevented the growth of the Revolution by mobilizing world opinion to make it impossible for the Revolution to rear its head.

Many patriots were killed during the turbulent years of reactionary rule in Ghana. An abortive military coup launched by three young army lieutenants in 1967 to stop the gamblings of the reactionary military officers in Ghana ended in failure. The three leaders were immediately arrested and Lieutenant Arthur and Lieutenant Yeboah were later executed while Lieutenant Osei Poku was given a long prison sentence.

On 17th June 1945, Chairman Mao Tse-Tung, while addressing a memorial meeting of those who had been killed in the Chinese revolution, declared:

All reactionaries try to stamp out revolution by mass murder, thinking that the greater their massacre, the weaker the revolution. But contrary to this reactionary wishful thinking, the fact is that the more the reactionaries resort to massacre, the greater the strength of the revolution and the nearer the reactionaries approach their doom. This is an inescapable law.

The people of Ghana have never given up their struggle against reaction despite the killings of those who rose up in revolt against the oppressive system.

An Italian philosopher once declared, "There is nothing more difficult to take in hand, more perilous to conduct or more uncertain in its success than to take the lead in the introduction of a new order of things." That saying shows precisely the task that will face the young revolutionaries in Ghana. Revolution, as Chairman Mao says in one of his works, can never be a dinner party. The Ghana Revolution is bound to be attacked and defended ferociously. The reactionaries are going to attempt large-scale disruptions of the revolution; already a national committee for the restoration of democracy has been established by some members of the banned Peoples National Party of Ghana in exile in opposition to the Ghana Revolution. A military wing of the committee has also been launched in London with two of Jerry Rawlings' former associates in the Armed Forces Revolutionary Council, Major Boakye-Djan and Major Poku-Mensah, as members. The aim is to invade Ghana and destroy, what to the P.N.P members, appears to be a teenage revolution. The struggle in the days to come will be fierce in Ghana. Jerry Rawlings and his associates must use the lessons of Nkrumah's rule and the teachings of Nkrumaism to guide the revolution they have proclaimed.

Nkrumaism is the guiding socialist philosophy of the African Revolution. Nkrumah and Nkrumaism represent the struggle for a free and democratic Africa. Struggle never ends, as Leo Huberman has put it, "It is a law of life".

It will indeed be tragic if, in the final analysis, the young revolutionaries in Ghana have merely toyed with a revolution.

Failure of the revolution as I mentioned earlier could spell a permanent disaster for democratic forces in Ghana, nay all of Africa, and it could deal very deadly blows on Nkrumaism.

2
Busia and Acheampong

Colonel Ignatius Kutu Acheampong had a fine opportunity of steering Ghana's political course on the progressive road but he unfortunately lacked the will, the courage, the enthusiasm and the drive to carry this through. He was a gifted ruler who wanted to make a success of a very difficult situation, but he allowed opportunism to take control of his reason. He opened the gates of his regime to flatterers and sycophants. In the end, he was deserted by all, denied by all and left alone to suffer the agonies and the pains of his six and a half years of misplaced opportunities.

On 13th January 1972, Colonel Acheampong gladdened the hearts of many people in the world by the dawn overthrow of the regime of Professor Kofi Abrefa Busia. The coup was hailed in all parts of Africa, because it was seen as a coup to restore the old glories of

Ghana. When he announced the overthrow of Kofi Busia and the termination of the neo-colonial puppet government of the Progress Party, the people of Ghana and Africa jumped for joy not because they were happy to witness yet another eruption from the military barracks but because their hopes were raised as to the coming of the great leader of Africa, the leader whose image once made the imperialists tremble and fear, the man whose voice thundered the rhythm of the great African Revolution — Kwame Nkrumah.

However, the initial statement made by Kutu Acheampong did not portray him as a serious-minded ruler. At first he told the world that both Kwame Nkrumah and Kofi Busia were free to enter Ghana but the two would have to answer charges preferred against them. Later, he joined hands with the democratic forces in Ghana who had wanted to see the golden return of Nkrumah and Nkrumaism.

Many people felt that the Ghana revolution would be proclaimed by Kutµ Acheampong but Nkrumaism was later betrayed by him. It is pertinent to reconstruct Ghana's political history in order to understand clearly the rise and fall of Acheampong's regime.

When Nkrumah fell, the British and the American imperialists came fully to power in Ghana, represented by the Busia-Harley-Afrifa-Kotoka clique. The history of Ghana took a new but pitiable turn. A military junta was formed under the leadership of General Ankrah who had been retired by Kwame Nkrumah on grounds of Ankrah's brazen incompetence as a military officer. The regime of General Ankrah was so repressive that at least three thousand people were said to have fled the country while about five hundred people died.

The first attempt to overthrow the neo-colonial puppet regime of the National Liberation Council was made on the morning of 17th April 1967. A dramatic announcement on Ghana radio said the N.L.C. had been disbanded and that a Lieutenant Colonel Asante, the then Commander of Ghana's parachute battalion based in Sekondi Takoradi, had take over power. Another snappy announcement coming about thirty minutes later said the coup had been crushed.

It was later learnt that the counter-coup was led by three young army lieutenants at the head of some one hundred and twenty men of the Recce Squadron based some few miles outside Accra. The leaders of the putsch were Lieutenants Samuel Arthur, Moses Yeboah and Second Lieutenant Osei Poku.

At the trial of these three bold and patriotic young men, they told the five man military tribunal that the Harley-Afrifa-Ankrah clique had no political mandate from the people to govern. They accused the leaders of the N.L.C. of corruption, and Lieutenant Arthur courageously told the tribunal that what he and his group had done was exactly the same thing done by the N.L.C. in 1966 in staging a coup d'etat. He said the only difference was that while theirs failed, the one of the N.L.C. succeeded. Consequently Lieutenants Arthur and Yeboah were executed at the Teshie firing range (some few yards away from the spot where Afrifa was himself to be later executed in 1979). Lieutenant Osei Poku was given thirty years imprisonment.

The abortive coup attempt of the young lieutenants was the first major attempt by democratic forces in Ghana to stop the aimless and purposeless gamble of the members of the National Liberation Council. Jerry Rawlings was to later come in 1979 to give real meaning to the anti-corruption coup of Lieutenants Arthur, Yeboah and Osei Poku in the two dramatic military events of 1st May and 4th June 1979.

In August 1969, in one of the most openly rigged elections ever held in Africa, the N.L.C. cleverly paved the way for the emergence of Kofi Busia. Prior to that election, members of Nkrumah's Convention People's Party (C.C.P.) were forbidden to seek political offices within the existing political parties and were banned from contesting the elections. There was an immediate reaction against this measure. The influential *Legon Observer* criticised the measure in an editorial written in the May edition of 1968. The editorial stated *inter alia*:

> The Political Parties Decree represents an important new departure in the development of the political process in the country. The decree disqualifies a further category of the C.C.P. from holding office in any political party or belong, or becoming

members of parliament, the main purpose of which is clearly to exclude these men from active political life of the country. But above all, this action illustrates the crucial weakness and failure of the N.L.C. policies towards the ex C.P.P., witness the paradoxical inconsistency, the unaccountable exception and the influence of personalities.

It is to be hoped this is the final effort for any further change or changes in response to further developments which should be condemned as sign of arbitrariness in decision, a lack of sensibility, a penchant towards confusion and a self inflicted vote of no confidence.

Busia was eventually manipulated into power and Ghana embarked on a senseless political safari which eventually terminated on 31st December 1981 with Jerry Rawlings proclaiming the birth of the Ghana Revolution.

Ghana's economy had been totally destroyed and Busia heightened the reactionary policy of the Afrifa administration in ordering Africans out of Ghana.

I remember that on the 21st of December, 1971, I was invited to the Ghana High Commission in Lagos by Ghana's then High Commissioner in Nigeria, Major General Emmanuel Aferi, who had been Chief of Defence Staff in Nkrumah's Ghana before the 1966 coup. It was he, Nkrumah had appointed in the place of General Ankrah. General Aferi had invited me for some discussion connected with a pamphlet I had just released then titled "Military Intervention in African Politics." In that small pamphlet I had written the following while describing the political events in Ghana:

> With the coup against Nkrumah and with the emergence of a ruler, Kofi Busia, who is more English than the English man himself, Ghana has been returned to the gambling house of colonialism and capitalist oppression and unless Nkrumah is returned, the country may never come out of it again.

General Aferi had called me to his office to dispute this verdict with me. I remember that at a stage during the discussion, I politely told the

Busia and Acheampong 15

Commissioner that it was not necessary for the two of us to continue debating a dead matter as all was soon to be over in Ghana. He looked at my face, shook his head, had a reluctant handshake with me, bought ten copies of my pamphlet and we both parted company.

On 13th of January, 1972 my prediction came true. On that morning, Colonel Ignatius Kutu Acheampong, then a forty-one year old Sandhurst trained army officer, Major Selormey, Major Agbo and Major Kwame Baah put an end to the regime of Professor Kofi Abrefa Busia.

Some have claimed that the major reason why Acheampong overthrew the Busia-led Progress Party government was as a result of a cut in the budget of the Armed forces. The soldiers could not bear the cut and so planned a coup to remove the man they considered instrumental to the decision. No matter the reason, it was clear to all observers of Ghana's politics that the Busia government was such a despicable and reactionary government that an immediate surgical operation was needed to terminate such a regime.

Acheampong's coup against Busia was a welcome relief to the people of Ghana, for the country had lost virtually all the beauty of her history under Busia's regime and a country once noted for her radical Pan-African revolutionary activities became a major centre of imperialist reaction and machination. Busia was a member of the unholy triumvirate (including Houphouet Boigny of Ivory Coast and President Tolbert of Liberia) that started the Dialogue Club in Africa. It was the triumvirate's contention that the racist masters of South Africa must be engaged in discussions. It was Busia's contention that Africans could never win the war against apartheid on the battlefield. In essence, Busia was denying armed struggle as a legitimate weapon in the hands of fighters for national liberation. Ghana, which had been dubbed the nursery of African "subversives" by imperialism as a result of her total and absolute commitment to liberation struggles in Africa under the Kwame Nkrumah regime, became a different country entirely. South African planes were having a field day at the Accra Airport that was infamously christened the Kotoka International Airport by the N.L.C. after the abortive coup of

Lieutenant Arthur. South African goods were also openly on display in the streets of Accra.

By 13th January 1972, it was apparent that the regime of Busia would collapse. All Ghana's democratic forces including the members of Nkrumah's young pioneers who had now graduated from the universities heightened the struggles for people's democracy and so prepared the grounds for the liquidation of a reactionary terrorist regime.

Professor Kofi Abrefa Busia did not only succeed in subjecting Ghana to brutal and barbaric tyranny, but he also succeeded in treacherously selling Ghana's interests to his imperialist backers. The dedicated Ghanaian patriots resisting the sadistic rule of Busia turned Nkrumah's writings into the bible of the struggle. They were constantly guided by Nkrumah's New Year resolutions of 1965 which ended on the following decisive tone:

> Don't use your position to enrich yourself,
> Don't be afraid to do what is right,
> Be modest in your way of living,
> Be honest
> Don't embezzle public funds or misuse public property
> Watch your class enemies.

Ghanaian students and patriotic citizens remained undaunted in their efforts to rid their country of a permanent menace. The opportunity came on 13th January 1972 with the military action of Acheampong.

The Colonel Acheampong's coup indeed offered Ghanaians fresh hopes that a beautiful tomorrow had come for Ghana. Acheampong however gambled with a million dollar chance before him to make a revolution. This mistake was to later cost him his life.

13th January, 1972

Speaking to a Ghanaian delegation to Ivory Coast in June 1966, Houphouet Boigny made this remark:

Our peoples, once united by all sorts of affinities, and then divided by the hateful policy of Kwame Nkrumah are henceforth brothers, struggling for the same ideal and the same goal of happiness in liberty. Today our people have two enemies Kwame Nkrumah and Sekou Toure.

Addressing his "Conseil National" shortly after the visit, Boigny also said to his eternal tragedy, "revolution only flowers in a soil of misery". Nkrumah and Sekou Toure were dubbed enemies by Houphouet Boigny simply because the two leaders would not sacrifice the interests of Africa on mere pots of porridge. While Nkrumah, Sekou Toure, Modibo Keita, Mohammed Ben Barka and Abdel Gamal Nasser were resisting imperialism with their sweat and resources, Houphouet Boigny, Leopold Sedar Senghor and Busia were busy consolidating imperialist positions in Africa. It was clear to all that a revolutionary Ghana that would once again have a semblance of Nkrumah's era would never be tolerated by imperialism and its lackeys. Acheampong saw this clear sign and instead of seizing the hour, exploiting the revolutionary zeal and enthusiasm of the young Ghanaians that were eagerly looking for a progressive change, and positively moving Ghana forward on the socialist road, his purpose degenerated and collapsed to naked ambition. The beauty of his coup d'etat was to vanish as the years rolled by. Eventually, he was deserted by all, even his own colleagues of the National Redemption Council.

Acheampong started well by embarking on a massive agricultural programme. He mobilised all Ghanaians back to the farms and it was during this era that Colonel Bernasko, who was later to lead a political party in Ghana, made his mark. The Ghana Fishing Corporation was given a boost and Ghana once again bubbled with revolutionary enthusiasm and fervour. University students took the lead in the new scheme of things being initiated by Acheampong. The students were the first to obey the clarion call of Acheampong to all Ghanaians to return to the farms.

Acheampong also did very well with the burial of Kwame Nkrumah. Before Nkrumah died in Rumania on 27th April 1972,

Acheampong had privately sent Nkrumah's son, Francis Nkrumah, to Conakry, Guinea to ask the old man whether he would wish to return back to Ghana. Kwame Nkrumah was already weak by the time this visit was made and when Nkrumah died, Acheampong ensured that a fitting state burial was given to the man who had inspired millions of Africans.

The imperialists and their Ghanaian lackeys were so afraid that another Nkrumah had arrived on Ghana's political scene that they immediately unleashed a spate of rumours and gossips to discredit the Acheampong regime before it damaged their position. Shortly after a Nigerian Afro-beat musician, Fela Anikulapo Kuti, was invited to play at Accra by the Acheampong regime, rumour went out that Acheampong was a Nigerian from Fela's home town, Abeokuta. Imperialism had cleverly matched Fela's surname Kuti with Acheampong's middle name Kutu to convince the people of the doubtful citizenship of Acheampong. The rumour was so strong that official statements were issued several times from the Osu Castle (the seat of government) to deny the rumour. Throughout the six and a half years of Ignatius Kutu Acheampong's rule, he never ventured out of Ghana. The farthest point he went was Aflao, the border town between Ghana and Togo.

The Nkrumah old guards who later formed the People's National party owed their return to Ghana to Acheampong. He rehabilitated several of those who had fled Ghana after the overthrow of Kwame Nkrumah in 1966. However Acheampong was later to exploit for his own selfish advantage the revolutionary consciousness of some of these men. The national Charter of Redemption which was the ideological framework of Acheampong's phoney revolution was worked out by some of these Nkrumah old guards.

General Acheampong brought Kwame Nkrumah's widow, Madame Fathia Nkrumah, and her children back to Ghana and resettled them at state expense. He also ordered a new statue of Kwame Nkrumah to be placed at the old Polo ground where the Osagyefo proclaimed the independence of Ghana. He encouraged the establishment of the Kwame Nkrumah Memorial lectures at the

University of Cape Coast. The second in the series of these lectures was delivered in 1976 by Chief Obafemi Awolowo, a radical socialist politician in Nigeria. It was also Acheampong's regime that financed the three international conferences held on the life and times of Kwame Nkrumah under the auspices of the Ghana Peace and Solidarity Council chaired by Kwesi Ghapson (who later served as Adviser to Acheampong). I was privileged to have been one of the participants at the third international seminar held at the Kwame Nkrumah Conference Centre, Accra in April, 1976.

General Acheampong had genuine motives initially but they soon degenerated in the face of his inordinate ambition and his inability to curb the large-scale corruption of some elements in his administration. Ideologically, Acheampong was far from the Afrifa-Kotoka clique. He realised the importance of mass mobilisation in furthering support of the people for a regime. To this end, he encouraged the growth and development of anti-imperialist organisations in Ghana. He however failed to utilise these organisations decisively when it became clear to him that they could become powerful enough to successfully challenge his leadership eventually. Some of the organisations that received open encouragement from Acheampong included the Ghana Peace and Solidarity Council, and the African Youth Command (the author is the current Continental President General of the organisation). Acheampong gave substantial monetary assistance for the expansion of these organisations but they were used by Acheampong only at moments most convenient for his own selfish motivations. These anti-imperialist organisations were loud in their support for Acheampong's "union government" which was another method for decreeing him as the life ruler of Ghana. (I would like to mention here that some of the left wing organisations in Ghana have, since the coup of Acheampong in 1972, been used by succeeding military regimes to popularise their regimes. The seeming opportunism of these organisations will no doubt constitute a major barrier to the Ghana Revolution. I intend to discuss this seriously in the chapter dealing with the Ghana revolution itself.) Since the overthrow of Kwame

Nkrumah, many of Ghana's left wing organisations have assumed a survivalist character which has not helped the course of the revolutionary movement in the country. Circumstances must have forced them to this unfortunate situation, but it is my honest contention that it is ideologically wrong for socialist forces to continue to compromise positions simply to save their skins. Chairman Mao was right when he said that if Unity is sought through struggle it will live but if it is sought through compromise and yielding of positions it will perish. Ghana's left wing organisations since 1972 have compromised with various military regimes and have thereby compromised the Ghana Revolution itself. These organisations have now fused into the C.P.P. The only groups that consistently maintained the socialist character of the Ghana Revolution are the militant National Union of Ghana Students (NUGS) and the C.P.P. (Overseas branch in London), publishers of the radical journal *The Dawn* I will be dealing extensively with this factor later in the book.

The deliberate use of Nkrumah's image, methods and ideas by General Acheampong ignited the hatred of some of the imperialist countries against his regime. The greatest offence Acheampong committed against imperialist interests was when, at the very last minute, he cancelled the proposed visit of the former American Secretary of State, Henry Kissinger in 1976. The Kissinger advance party had already arrived in Accra and all arrangements had been concluded before the visit was cancelled.

I was in Accra at the time and I can attest at first hand to the elaborate arrangements already made both by Ghanaian and White House security organisations on the Kissinger visit before it was cancelled on the grounds that General Acheampong was sick with a boil. The Continental Hotel in Accra had already been completely taken over. No other guests had been allowed to lodge in the hotel for two weeks prior to the date of arrival of Henry Kissinger. The carpets, tables, bed linens and everything imaginable in the hotels rooms had been changed.

And while these elaborate arrangements were going on, General Acheampong bowed down to the revolutionary pressures of the

National Union of Ghana Students (NUGS), one of the most highly militant student organisations in Africa, and the Kissinger visit was cancelled.

The American Ambassador in Accra, Miss Shirley Temple Black, was immediately recalled to the United States and America became openly hostile against the Acheampong regime. Unfortunately, General Acheampong's narrow view of the complexities of modern international politics which are clearly cemented on an ideological struggle between capitalist and socialist forces caused him to wave off the tragic consequences of open-handedly taking on America. His mad ambition to get his regime legitimised through a bogus union government proposal opened the gates to imperialist lackeys who kept on advising him until he (Acheampong) met his political doom in the hands of his own colleagues. This naivety also finally cost him his life and also led to the collapse of his paper revolution. The details of Acheampong's naivety are supplied in the next chapter.

3
The Collapse of Acheampong's "Revolution"

I know Ghana very well. As a convinced Nkrumaist, I have always taken very keen interest in Ghana's affairs. I was there in Accra on 13th January 1978 when General Acheampong celebrated the sixth anniversary of his "revolution". I had been invited to the celebrations as a special guest of the "African Youth Command".

Quite ironically the man who commanded the parade of the memorable sixth anniversary of Acheampong's coup was the late General Odartey Wellington.

That day, I predicted to my associates with whom I shared the day that it looked to me that Ghana was on the verge of disaster. Some shared my views while others felt otherwise. On 5th July 1978 the end of Acheampong's regime was announced and it was Odartey Wellington that finally nailed the coffin of Acheampong's regime.

Acheampong chased his own shadow for the period of his rule. He trusted no one and he eventually became a prisoner of Zenda. The security of the entire state was not his concern; he was more concerned with his own personal security. Acheampong spent the best part of his administration arresting opponents of his regime. He survived several coup attempts, both real and imaginary. Brigadier Kattah was declared a wanted person in 1975 after having been discovered to be plotting a coup. Dr. Kofi Awoonor, a lecturer of the University of Cape Coast, was later arrested and accused of aiding and abetting the escape of Brigadier Kattah to Ivory Coast.

Mr. Kojo Botsio, Alhaji Ayarna and John Tettegah were arrested and tried for plotting a coup against the Acheampong regime. They were sentenced to death but their sentences were later commuted to life imprisonment. They were released by Jerry Rawlings after the 4th June, 1979 coup. Alex Hammah, a trade unionist, was also sentenced to death for plotting a coup against Acheampong. All these men were said to have contacted late General Robert Kotei for their various coup attempts against the Acheampong regime.

Acheampong's fear for his personal security and safety also led him to drop the three young Majors, Selormey, Agbo and Kwame Baah, who had helped him stage the 1972 coup from the Supreme Military Council (SMC) in 1975. The young majors consequently tendered their resignations from the Ghana Army.

A clearer picture of the arbitrary arrests that were perpetrated by the Acheampong's regime can be seen from a notice published in the *Daily Graphic* of Ghana by B. J. Da Rocha on the sad case of Moses Ambrose Da Rocha. Part of the notice reads:

> ...In July 1972 my brother was arrested from his house one evening by officers from the Special Branch. He was subsequently taken to Michel Camp and locked up in a guard room. It is not quite clear at what precise moment it happened; but while there my brother was subjected to the most brutal and degrading torture. The nails of his fingers and toes were pulled out. His testicles were almost crushed. His thighs and his back were covered with the most frightening bruises. His ribs were

kicked in and his lungs collapsed. He died in agony. At the time this took place, I was in detention in Ussher Fort. I was denied permission to attend his burial but photographs of his mutilated body were taken by my sister and I was able when I came out of prison to see the photographs. I have still got them.

There was no reason at all why my brother should have been arrested. The authorities must have known that I was in prison so they should not have mistaken him for me. He was not and had never been actively engaged in politics. There was no evidence that he had been involved in any attempted coup. Yet someone must have made a report on him and someone must have given the order for his arrest and someone must have ordered him to be treated with the brutality which caused his death.

The fate of Da Rocha portrayed the Gestapo-styled adminstration promoted by Acheampong. In the end, the people of Ghana revolted against the regime, defying arrest and waging relentless struggles against Acheampong's opportunist "Union Government" proposal.

Despite daily arrests of opponents of the regime, Acheampong was forced out of power by the persistent actions of the Ghana people. Acheampong's regime also collapsed because he was not in a position to curb the corruption of his lieutenants. One of the memorable incidents of corruption during the Acheampong era was the R. T. Briscoe scandal of 1979. A senior journalist of the *Ghanaian Times* was able to unearth a scandal involving top military officers with R. T. Briscoe, a multinational company with a branch in Accra. Acheampong later retired four top military officers including the then Commander of the Ghana Airforce, Major General Beausoleil.

Despite the scarcity of essential commodities in Ghana, a few privileged persons who were close to the regime had these commodities in sufficient quantity. The extravagance and squandermania of some of the lieutenants of Ignatius Acheampong were also responsible for a complete alienation of the vast majority of the people of Ghana from his regime. By June 1978, it was apparent that the economy of Ghana would collapse.

Perhaps the greatest undoing of General Acheampong was the

attempt he made to sentence Ghana to an indefinite military rule under his absolute and total leadership. The people, who had passed through turbulent political storms since the struggle for independence began and had successfully weathered through them, were not impressed by the chameleonic character of Acheampong. By 1977, open demands were being made by the Ghanaian people for a return to normal democratic rule.

Acheampong's answer to the people's call for an immediate return to normal democratic rule was his Union Government proposal. It was his contention that party politics had failed to unite the people of Ghana and had, in fact, divided them very badly.

Acheampong advocated a union government which was another name for a fascist no-party state programme. He was rebuffed by the people and despite his clever manipulations of the referendum held in April 1978 to record a fifty-four percent support of the Ghana people for the idea, the people pressed on until the idea was completely abandoned by the military authorities.

Acheampong's idea was not however defeated without a fight. General Acheampong, through the organisations he had created, campaigned throughout the length and breadth of Ghana for the adoption of "Union Government". The Ghana Peace and Solidarity Council, the African Youth Command, and an organisation called "The Friends" were the official propagandists of this reactionary idea. The moral licentiousness that characterised the operations of "The Friends" with its club house on the Accra-Winneba road did serious harm to Acheampong's image. In essence, "The Friends" was an organisation of businessmen who were loyal to Ignatius Acheampong. Unfortunately these were strong anti-imperialist organisations serving reactionary ends.

Acheampong's agents infiltrated into nearly all professional groups. The Ghana Bar Association was soon to have a democratic wing that rallied around Acheampong's Union Government idea. Acheampong was a very clever officer who tried to use revolutionary intellectuals and organisations to project himself as the nation's undisputed leader. He unfortunately had no ideological orientation and his inordinate ambition was to lead to a vicious opposition that finally dismissed his leadership. Genuine revolutionaries in Ghana had to go into alliance with extreme right wing groups in the fight against Acheampong.

The National Union of Ghana Students (NUGS), association of Recognised Professional Bodies and other organisations came together to fight the Union Government proposal. It was a most bitter struggle. University students all over Ghana abandoned their campuses and pledged never to return for their studies until the Union Government idea was abandoned and a programme of return to normal democratic rule was accepted by Acheampong. The idea died an unceremonious death after the sudden but long expected removal from office of Acheampong by his colleages of the National Redemption Council.

Three documents among several others that were circulated by the various organisations that fought Acheampong on his Union Government proposal are hereby published for posterity. The content of the struggle for democracy in Ghana between 1977 and 1978 has shown that it will be extremely difficult for Ghana to ever embrace a totalitarian fascist regime. The Ghanaians, through their long years of struggle, will never permit a situation where the people will be bamboozled with mere rhetoric and their lives sentenced to irredeemable frustration and despair. Jerry Rawlings and his colleagues of the PNDC will have to study very closely the history of the anti-Union Government struggle in Ghana between 1976 and 1978 as a guide to the course they will want to chart for the Ghana revolution. Any mistake may make all of them go the Acheampong way.

National Union of Ghanian Students

Open Letter to Mr Kwame Gyawu-Kyem
(Editor of Times)

June 17, 1977

Mr Kwame Gyawu-Kyem
c/o *Ghanaian Times*
Accra

Dear Mr. Gyawu-Kyem,
 The students of Ghana wish to inform you that we are aware of the hopeless manner in which you have handled the *Ghanaian Times* so far.
 Your activities after the May 13 historic countrywide students demonstrations have made the hitherto doubtful ones become convinced of your real nature: You are an enemy of the people!
 When one reads your editorial columns one doesn't know what to wonder at most – your ignorance, unscrupulousness, dishonesty or your illiteracy? On May 13 1977 you told the whole world that we students demonstrated over food problems on our campuses. As a result you accused us of being selfish, reactionary, that "the leadership *has gone haywire*", our "*judgement gone rustic*", etc.
 Surprisingly you couldn't publish a single picture of any demonstrator bearing a placard that we want food for ourselves.
 We feel very sorry for you that after having yourself promoted to Supervising Editor you are exhibiting such immaturity as will not be expected of an editor of a secondary school magazine.
 Since the suggestion of the idea of Union Government, you have displayed your illiteracy to the public well enough and we are greatly concerned that you are still not ashamed at exposing your ignorance.
 You have published before that Union Government is a novel idea, that it is to have evolved out of our tradition, that it will be on non-party basis and that people will come from near and far to see.

The Collapse of Acheampong's "Revolution" 29

However, when a lawyer said at a symposium in Accra that Union Government is strange and has not been practised anywhere before, you wanted to prove him wrong. In this attempt you wrote that British coalition governments were forms of Union Government. But Kwame, British coalitions have always been by at least *two political parties. They were therefore not non-party*. Here, poor Kwame, you exhibited your illiteracy to the elementary school pupils. Or did you forget that Union Government is supposed to be on non-party basis?

That was not all. Your editorial of June 10 1977 captioned "A Revolution is not a Tea Party", laid your ignorance bare.

Before we tackle your editorial comment, we would like to know why you sometimes quote Comrade Mao Tse-Tung at all? Was it because of that single booklet you were given when you visited China? You seem to be quoting the same things everyday. Is it because that is the only revolutionary piece you have read? You are yourself anti-socialist and quoting Chairman Mao's socialist ideas to suit your reactionary intentions makes you look like a monkey in man's clothing.

We were amused by that editorial. That day, everyone was asking who gave you that Diploma in Journalism. Yet you are the one who accused the students of not knowing anything, and that even before we have finished reading a single book we already think we know too much. But it appears to us that in your case, you do not read at all.

Even if you did not earlier know the meanings of "revolution", "reactionary", "progressive", etc, the sections you quoted should have guided you. You wrote: "A revolution is an insurrection, an act of violence by which one class overthrows another." Since you have been defending the 1972 coup as a "revolution", we would like you to tell us which class overthrew another in 1972?

As far as we are concerned the 1972 coup was an intra-class conflict – a fight among members of the bourgeois class. This is because, by correct definition, the bourgeois class includes the top hierarchy of the army, the top brass of the civil service, the chiefs, the so-called businessmen, the defenders of bourgeois law and that section of intellectuals that has aligned itself with imperialism or its agents. Mr Gyawu-Kyem, you fall into the last category. To crown it all, Comrade Fidel Castro said earlier this year that "A Revolution is not achieved through a coup d'etat". We hope you will uphold Comrade Castro's dissertation on "revolution".

In distinguishing the people's friends from their enemies, you wrote that, "the enemies are all those in league with imperialism – the bureaucrat and the reactionary, are an enemy of the people."

This analysis clearly shows that you did not understand what you wrote yourself; otherwise you wouldn't have condemned yourself so much. That is why it is prudent to acknowledge that "*A little learning is dangerous*" and it is always advisable in such cases to "*drink deep or taste not*".

By your own definition, you are not a revolutionary; do not mislead yourself into thinking that merely growing a beard makes you a revolutionary.

You are always full of praises for the *little school children of Soweto* for their initiative, etc., yet whenever university students act, you claim that "disgruntled politicians" and "*foreign powers*" are behind. You think that we students cannot think for ourselves. But you must admit that it was a then first year student of the University of Ghana who coached you into opposing the visit of Mr Henry Kissinger to Ghana last year.

The motive behind the May 13 action is best described by a quotation in one of this year's issue of "Gramma" about a student uprising.

> These commitments were a reflection of anti-imperialist militancy, continuity of the purest traditions of the struggle of ... students and identification with the masses and their aspirations. It meant confrontation of the oppressors of the people, defying the ire of dictatorship, transforming ideas into deeds, tempering the will in revolutionary principles. It meant defying death and being willing to carry the supreme act of patriotism: Giving one's life for the country.

For us students we live by the saying that "*If we should fall, let our blood point the way to freedom. Because whether or not our action is successful, the commotion it will give rise to, will help us along the road to victory. But it is the people's action that will be decisive in obtaining it.*"

While ending this letter, we advise you to learn hard to justify your promotion to Supervising Editorship. You need to improve.

Yours sincerely

Sgd.
Kwasi Adu
(National Secretary)

Association of Recognised Professional Bodies

Issue: Vol. 1, No. 1 4th July, 1977

The Vague Time Table

Fellow Ghanaians, you will remember that at a meeting held on 23rd June, 1977, the Association of Recognised Professional Bodies passed a Resolution in which it called upon the Government of the SMC to resign and hand over to a Presidential Commission because that Government had shown by various acts and omissions that it had become increasingly incompetent to govern this country.

In that Resolution, again the Association warned that if by Friday, 1st July, 1977 the Government had not complied with that demand to resign, all members of the Professional Bodies within the Association of Recognised Professional Bodies shall without further notice withdraw all their services to the general public.

In a national broadcast on 1st July, 1977, the Head of State and Chairman on the SMC, General Acheampong attempted to answer some of the issues raised in the Resolution of the Association of Professional Bodies.

It is the belief of the Association, however, that this attempt was only meant to stall the action contemplated by the Association and did not effectively address itself to the problems presently plaguing our dear motherland.

It is unfortunate that it has become a regular feature in the political life of this country that whenever any individual or group of individuals out of national feeling criticise or oppose any move of the government in power, which they feel to be detrimental to the national interest, they are labelled as traitors, saboteurs or enemies of the revolution.

Here we are again with it being alleged that certain groups in the community have sought to disturb orderly development and disrupt the efforts of the SMC government at national building. The Head of State in his broadcast said these people are doing this upon the pretext that food is difficult to come by and that the proposed Union Government is aimed at perpetuating military cum police rule in Ghana.

On this point one would ask if anybody in Ghana today, who is aware of what is going on and is conscious of the living conditions of the people, would say that it is a pretext that food is difficult to come by in this country. Is it not true that Ghanaians are starving because they cannot get their basic staple foods, let alone the foreign ones? Is the cost of food in the country today not above what the average Ghanaian can afford? We state as a fact that a number of our Secondary schools were forced to close down ahead of schedule because there was not enough food for the students.

Parents even now face the likelihood of paying increased boarding fees because some schools have threatened not to reopen for the next academic year if fees are not increased.

Now, how does one reconcile the Head of State's statement that the allegation of food shortage is a pretext with his admission that after 2 years of no rain coupled with the oil crisis which led to global inflation, it is not surprising that we in Ghana, as others elsewhere, should suffer from shortage of food and other imported items.

It is the opinion of this Association that the S.M.C. government cannot take shelter under the failure of rain and the oil crisis to escape liability and blame for the unprecedented food shortage and famine which Ghanaians are now experiencing. The government has displayed a serious lack of foresight and responsibility.

One would have thought that when the rains failed in the first year and repeated the following year, the government would have foreseen the imminent consequences and taken appropriate steps to forestall them by importing some food far in advance. On the other hand what did we see? Under the nose of the government we embarked on large scale exportation of the little food we had and continued until last month. How can a government escape blame for such lack of foresight and negligence?

Now on the Union Government proposal. If the government wanted Ghanaians to have a free hand in determining the form of government they want, why did it not say so from the start? Why did it lay it down that the basis of Union government shall be a composition of the *army*, the *police* and *civilians*?

Ghanaians are now being told that the whole question of Union government will be subjected to a national referendum to enable them to decide whether they like the Union government and if so, in what form? For the first time they are being told that they can exclude the army and the police if they do not want them in the government.

As is always the case, the mass media, including information services vans will be touring the whole country to canvass for Union Government as suggested by the government, before the country goes to a referendum. The question one wants to ask is how can we guarantee that the opposite view to Union Government will be equally and fairly put before the people. Already, the mass media and organised demonstrations have started the campaign for Union Government.

The government cannot claim to have been fair and unbiased in its distribution of the national cake. The Ghana Chamber of Commerce has always asked that those issued import licences should have their names published with the amount against their names, but the government has never been able to do this just because selected people have had more than their fair share. If this allegation is denied, then we challenge the government to come out with a list of import licence allocation for the people to see.

In view of the above, this Association hereby reaffirms its resolution of 23rd June, 1977, that unless the Government of the S.M.C. resigns and hands over power as stated, all its members will withdraw their services from the public accordingly.

Our Revolution – An Appraisal

With the ensuing dissolution of the SMC regime, it has become necessary for a forethought to be given on the type of men we need to have to govern us and the nature of government we are to have.

The Collapse of Acheampong's "Revolution" 35

The form of dissolution of the SMC is yet to be known, although it may take one of these: (a) either it may be ousted by a military coup or (b) by resignation or (c) by absorption into a Union Government[?]. Assuming it is shaped off by another military coup, the question which I ask is: Is the intelligentsia going into the streets like before with placards heralding the new military regime? Or shall we sit and accept promises of "redemption", "liberation", "salvation", or "revolution" and a "return to civilian rule" at a "future date"? Or shall we rather stand firmly and unequivocally denounce *any* military regime and demand their instant vamuse to the barracks so that rule and power is wielded by civilians?

What answers we give to these questions will indicate in what direction our revolution is going. Further it will attest to the sincerity of the values we predicate of our revolution. A further question here is: how enduring is our revolution? Are we in search of a fundamental transformation of the Ghanaian body politic towards heightened political awareness and ennobling social values or are we intent on overthrowing an effete regime without a corresponding elimination of the negative causative factors which makes the government unpopular?

It is necessary that we reflect on the goals of the revolution and prune it of "revolutionary idealism" lest we achieve the immediate objective without a corresponding success in other vital areas, viz: political awareness of the people; minimisation of corruptive tendencies in the body politic, restraint of power of the government in office and lastly institution of democratic principles. In short we should guard against effecting an ephemeral socio-political revolution.

For our revolution to be well anchored as to attain permanence, the intelligensia must serve notice to the military in terms as crystal clear as daylight that *never* repeat *never* shall the military be allowed to *rule* this *nation* again. That the right place for them is the barracks and war-front [Southern-Africa?]. The military have time and again, not only in Ghana, but in several countries the world over, especially Latin America, shown their *congenital incapability* to govern as effectively and prudently as they profess they can. With increasing taste of the "blood of power" it may become impossible in the near future for the military to cease wielding power in this country unless they are firmly checked. Unless checked now, the military will design it an act of condescension to comply with directives of a civilian government. They will adopt the supercilious and misconceived notion that they are infallible. Time has shown that a military government poses the perennial political problem of, "who will guard the guards?" To whom are they answerable? Experience has shown that to none are they answerable. If this be so then are they eligible to rule?

To *any* government in office, the intelligentsia must again serve notice that it will merit its respect and support if and only if, the government upholds, respects and defends these three fundamental values: *truth, freedom, justice*. That at such time as any or all of these values are in sufferance the government shall forfeit its right of existence and governance, and we the people shall reserve the right to choose a government of our liking that will abide by these three values.

Until such a time as the broad masses attain a certain degree of education and awareness, the fight for the creation of a healthy political system falls mostly on the shoulders of the intelligentsia. It is only when we succeed in making it known to the nation at large that the present revolution is one of values that it shall be possible for the masses to be aroused from their slumber, and for Ghana to really develop on the right political course it chooses. The permanence of a revolution of values namely *truth, freedom* and *justice*, lies in the transcendentalism of these values over the kaleidoscopic politics of mankind. Those who practice these values survive and flourish; those who neglect them stagnate and perish, for the values are eternal. It is this vision which we need to invest in our revolution.

To sum up this point, there must be no let up of the revolution until we succeed. Secondly we must not support *any* military government in Ghana because the military is not endowed with the prerequisites for good government. Thirdly, we should always fight for the safeguard and practice of the values of *truth, freedom* and *justice* by *any* government in office. Lastly we should be more practical in our identification with the broad masses with whom power lies. There is the temptation on our part to let rhetoric and dialectics get the better of us in our identification with the masses, this revolution not withstanding.

The future government should be a cadre of stalwarts in the realms of finance and economics, justice, security and foreign affairs. Granted the knowledge and experience of these stalwarts and backed by the intelligentsia, guided by the principles of *truth, freedom* and *justice*, and blessed by the goodwill of the people, desirous of a morally beautiful Ghana, a more prosperous Ghana, a more free Ghana, a more powerful Ghana and a more respectful Ghana, *nothing* repeat *nothing* shall stay the course of the success of the truest revolution ever launched in the history of our land.

Mankind
Oguaa Hall.

The above published documents show the high political consciousness that are found in Ghana. The PNP attempted to slow down the growth of radical thought and opinion just for a time because many of the democratic organisations wanted to give the party a chance to re-establish the authentic image of Nkrumah in Ghana. With the failure and the apparent impotence of the Peoples National Party to awaken the sleeping Ghanaian revolutionaries, the democratic organisations in Ghana, in collaboration with the University students, came together and fought out the party, paving the way for the second coming of Jerry John Rawlings.

Ignatius Kutu Acheampong was no doubt a clever military officer. He attempted to give a progressive image to his regime by his deliberate use of democratic and anti-imperialist organisations. He however did not believe in them and neither did he trust them. His understanding of the potentialities of progressive organisations should however be commended. It is very clear to me that had Acheampong succeeded with his Union Government affair, and had the Ghanaian people acquiesced to the idea without question, Acheampong would have unleashed on Ghana a fascist regime.

4
The Tragedy of Akuffo

A coup d'etat is a military affair directed against an existing regime with the view to removing that regime. A coup d'etat is no revolutionary action as what it merely succeeds in doing is forcibly changing the top governing section of the country and replacing individuals within the same class in power. The coup of 5th July, 1978 that ousted Ignatius Acheampong from power was a palace coup led by Acheampong's fellow members of the National Redemption Council. It was a total betrayal of Acheampong as Acheampong was sacrificed by his colleagues to calm down an extremely injured Ghanaian population. The removal of Acheampong, as events later turned out, rather than calming down the people, further charged them in their struggle for people's democracy in the country. The bankruptcy of the system perpetrated by Acheampong and his succesor Akuffo succeeded only in arousing the anger and bitterness of junior officers in Ghana's armed forces against their seniors. it was the belief of the junior officers that their senior colleagues who had ruled Ghana since 1966 had been largely responsible for the economic problems of Ghana as a result of their corruption.

Much ink was spilt in the Western press about the overthrow of the government of General Ignatius Kutu Acheampong of Ghana. Many of the news reports and features on the abrupt termination of Acheampong's rule were largely exaggerated while others did not actually analyse the events before and after the Akuffo move on Acheampong. I was later to investigate the full story of how the palace coup against Acheampong was effected about a month after the event. This was the full story of the palace coup as narrated to me in Accra in 1978 by keen observers of the situation.

On 5th July 1978, General Ignatius Kutu Acheampong left his Burma Camp residence for the Osu Castle (where he had his military headquarters) at about nine in the morning without having any slightest suspicion of the conspiracy already hatched against him. His ousters were already waiting for him at his office. Still not knowing what was in the offing, Acheampong was quoted to have jocularly asked his colleagues of the Supreme Military Council whom he had met waiting for his arrival: "Gentlemen, is this an invasion?" The unsmiling military officers were to politely ask General Acheampong for an immediate audience in his office. Also unknown to Acheampong was the fact that his personal guards had been changed that morning on the orders of General Odartey Wellington (then Brigadier).

Acheampong was subsequently asked to read and sign a proclamation which had already been prepared by his colleagues of the Supreme Military Council. The prepared text had contained his resignation as the Head of State of Ghana as well as his retirement from the Ghana armed forces in what was described as being "in the interest of peace and stability in Ghana." Ignatius Acheampong was said to have expressed very serious objections to the statement. He was also said to have violently accused his ousters of infidelity, and intrigue claiming that they were all jointly responsible for the acts of his government.

There were reported hot exchanges between the officers and Acheampong and at one stage he requested that it was better for the ousters to have him shot. The situation was said to have been saved when the then Commander of the Ghana air force, Air Vice-Marshal Boakyi, who incidentally came from the same area as Acheampong, spoke their native Twi language to Acheampong requesting him to sign the document. Air Vice-Marshal Boakyi was said to have convinced Acheampong of the need to yield to the demands of the revolting military officers.

Acheampong was immediately arrested after signing the declaration. He however refused to be flown in a waiting air force helicopter to the Presidential lodge at Akosombo which was to serve as his detention place. General Robert Kotei who was only briefed of the coup that very morning and who had also been a close associate of Acheampong since the 1972 coup offered the deposed leader his own car and guards. Acheampong was then driven to Akosombo Presidential lounge while the Air Force helicopter hovered in the air.

Within one year, Acheampong was to see the inside of four detention camps. he was moved from Akosombo Presidential lodge to Ho prison. He was later moved to a prison in Northern Ghana. His last detention camp was the Ussher fort prison where many of his own victims had suffered untold degradation and injustice.

Acheampong's ADC, Captain Asare, was also arrested with him and confined to Michel Camp in Tema. The military secretary to Acheampong, Major Adjei Ampofo, was retired from the armed forces and also confined to Michel Camp.

Two reasons were said to have been adduced by the revolting officers for the palace coup of 5th July 1978. The members of the Supreme Military Council were said to have bowed down to the pressures of the people of Ghana which had clearly indicated large-scale displeasure for the Head of State, General Acheampong. Secondly, at a meeting of the SMC held at Burma Camp on 1st July, 1978, the members of the council had accused Acheampong of surrounding himself with questionable characters. Acheampong was said to have been so highly annoyed by the charges levied against him by his colleagues that he had to walk out of the meeting. The members of the SMC then decided to act fast to effect his removal so as not to be the victims of an immediate purge themselves.

Some days after the removal of Acheampong, both General Utuka, the former Commander of the Border Guards, and General Robert Kotei, the former Commander of the Ghana Army (who were friends of Acheampong), were retired by the new government. No reasons were given for their retirement. Inside sources however told me in Accra that the retirement of the officers came after it become known that they were planning to overthrow the new military government headed by General Akuffo with the aid of the armoured unit of the Ghana Police. The Ghana Police, unlike its Nigerian counterpart, has an armoured unit that had been specially trained in Britain.

One interesting thing about the palace coup that ousted Acheampong from power was the fact that a British Battalion was in Ghana training with the Ghana army on certain new military hardware purchased by the Ghana army from Britain when the coup occurred. Some of the British soldiers were seen guarding the British Embassy in Accra on the morning of 5th July 1978 the day of the change of guards. It was a mere coincidence as there was nothing to show any British complicity with the coup that removed Acheampong from power.

Acheampong's mistakes were many as mentioned earlier in this book. He eventually made himself prisoner of the corrupt business interests whose principal trade is to flatter leaders in order to consolidate their reactionary position. I have mentioned the formation of "The Friends" organisation which was a front for business sycophants in Ghana masquerading as progressives to maintain their hold on position, power and influence within the Acheampong regime.

Another identifiable mistake of Acheampong was his naivety. Most military rulers in Ghana (including even Jerry Rawlings in 1979) have been guilty of this. Acheampong's Union Government lacked any ideological premise. It was an opportunist creation to bamboozle the people of Ghana into accepting a totalitarian fascist regime. Nkrumaists who were in support of Acheampong's tower of Babel had told me in Accra that if Acheampong had announced after the Union Government referendum on 30th March 1978 that the eventual goal of his regime would be the building of a socialist Ghana and if he had shown signs of his sincerity of purpose as regards this postulation, the events of 5th July 1978 would not have occurred. I disputed these contentions with them on the grounds that the Ghanaian people had been deceived for so long by Acheampong that any declaration of intention by him would have been branded by the people as a mere smokescreen.

Acheampong fell to the cult of personality and instead of pursuing correct revolutionary lines (as he pretended to love socialism) he started appeasing capitalist roaders who had succeeded in worming themselves into Osu Castle his seat of power.

It will be unfair however to write off the Kutu Acheampong regime. One of the laudable programmes and schemes he initiated while in power was the "Operation Feed Yourself" and on the eve of the coup that ousted him, he had called on the country's economists to go to Ivinasa to deliberate on how Ghana would survive her economic difficulties.

Immediately after the removal of Acheampong from power, General Akuffo was announced as the new military ruler of Ghana. Akuffo announced the commitment of his government to the liberation movements in Africa and also declared his intention to honour all Ghana's obligations to international organisations like the OAU and the UN. His domestic policies were however a continuation of Acheampong's policies with some small cosmetic changes. The Akuffo government, instead of announcing a total rejection of Union Government, announced to Ghanaians that the new government would be implementing the initial proposal of the Ad hoc Committee on Union Government established by Acheampong in 1977, that Ghana should have a national government based on no-party politics. The Ghana Bar Association and the students did not waste time in denouncing the Akuffo intention. They dubbed the national government of Akuffo as another name for Acheampong's Union Government. General Akuffo and his government later bowed to the people's wishes for the establishment of political parties and a clear cut programme for the return of Ghana to normal democratic rule. The Akuffo government announced to the people of Ghana that the country would return to normal democratic rule in September 1979. The preparations for this exercise were already progressing when the Rawlings drama unfolded in Ghana.

One must mention here that while Ghanaian citizens welcomed the removal of General Acheampong, a sizeable number of officers and men of the Ghana Army did not give support. While some of them felt Acheampong had been betrayed by his colleagues who were also guilty of crimes against the Ghana nation, some felt that the total removal of the entire SMC would save the image of the army. Attempts to remove the 5th battalion in Accra (a battalion formerly commanded by Acheampong) to another location after the July 5 coup failed as the officers and men of the battalion refused posting. Indiscipline immediately crept into the Ghana Army and Akuffo and his men were helpless in the situation.

The ten months of Akuffo's government were months of rumours, gossips, and political uncertainty. It was said that many of the members of the SMC (including Akuffo) were sleeping outside their homes. The Akuffo government became absolutely incapable of maintaining a firm grip on power in Ghana. The resultant effect of this was the panic noticeable in the execution of the programmes for Ghana's return to normal democratic rule. Akuffo and his men were simply hurrying on to hand over to a new regime, thereby saving their own necks.

At this stage, Jerry John Rawlings and some of his colleagues of the Ghana Air Force started to ruminate over the problems of Ghana. It was their view and contention that Ghana's political and economic problems were direct results of the mismanagement and maladministration by the past military regimes that had ruled Ghana since 1966. The young officers felt that the corruption of Ghana's top military elite was sickening to the high heavens. Ghana was poor but the wealth was being displayed in all pomposity and arrogance by Ghana's top military leaders. The young boys felt that a trial of past and present Ghana's military leaders was necessary in order to restore the prestige of the Ghana Army and instill confidence and hope in the minds of Ghana citizens.

Repeated declarations and commitments of the Akuffo administration to the programme of Ghana's return to normal democratic rule did not calm the young military officers. The young men wanted a total break with Ghana's reactionary and decadent past. Despite the activities of political parties permitted to operate by the Akuffo government, Jerry John Rawlings and his men continued with their plans to terminate the military chop-chop regime of Akuffo and put a permanent stop to the rule of musical comedy generals in Ghana.

On 15th May 1979, Lieutenant Jerry Rawlings and his young military friends struck. The coup bid by the young officers failed when they were unable to link up with their colleagues in the Army. Thereafter it was quite easy for General Odartey Wellington to move againt the coup plotters. Rawlings and his fellow conspirators were immediately arrested. The trial of Rawlings afforded him the opportunity of spelling out in detail the philosophy of his attempted military putsch.

The press coverage given to the proceedings of the Court martial later proved the undoing of the Ghana Government. Rawlings did not mince words in his trial in condemning the various military regimes that had ruled in Ghana accusing them of corruption, greed, avarice and injustice. The boldness and dynamism exhibited by Jerry Rawlings in his trial where he had given clear expression to the mood and feelings of the Ghanaian people were to serve as the prairie fire that was to engulf Ghana on 4th June 1979 ushering in the Movement and preparing the grounds for the eventual declaration of the Ghana Revolution.

4th June 1979

The arrest and subsequent trial of Jerry Rawlings after the May 15 event completely destroyed discipline within the armed forces. The frustration of the junior officers and other ranks against their senior officers heightened. A few days before the June 4 coup, strange posters started appearing in military barracks attacking the corruption of Ghana's military leaders and calling for the immediate release of Rawlings and his colleagues.

A committee known as "Save Rawlings Movement" was formed and headed by Major Poku-Mensah and Major Boakye Djan. The committee was made up of young military officers and other ranks in the Ghana Army.

On 3rd June 1979, Major Boakye Djan and some of the revolting junior officers visited the mother of Rawlings to intimate her with their desire to release Rawlings from prison. Major Boakye Djan, who later became the spokesman for the Armed Forces Revolutionary Council, was a known socialist-Nkrumaist. He was perhaps the only known ideological officer within the inner corps of the Armed Forces Revoltionary Council.

On 4th June 1979, the young officers and other ranks of the Ghana Army struck. Rawlings and his detained colleagues of the May 15th abortive coup were released and an announcement was made on Radio Ghana for all officers and men that support the coup to assemble at the El Wak stadium for a meeting at 11 a.m.

General Odartey Wellington, then the Commander of Ghana Army who had led a detachment of the army to crush the revolt, was shot dead at an ensuing battle for the control of Radio Ghana. The students of the University of Legon Accra were said to have acted as informants to the young coup makers as regards the movement of the officers and men loyal to the Akuffo government. Jerry Rawlings himself went into hiding after it appeared that Odartey Wellington was progressing in his attempt to crush the coup.

The meeting of the junior officers and men of the Ghana Army was finally held at about 4 p.m. on the day of the coup and there the Armed

Forces Revolutionary Council was born. New Commanders of the Ghana armed forces were also announced.

All members of Akuffo's Supreme Military Council were arrested. General Ignatius Kutu Acheampong, General Robert Kotei, General Utuka and General Akwasi Amansa Afrifa who were all retired military officers were also placed under arrest. They were subsequently tried for corruption and various acts of perfidy against the people of Ghana.

On 28th June 1979, General Akuffo, Air Vice-Marshal Boakyi, General Archeampong, and the naval commander were executed by firing squad. Soon after, General Akwasi Amansa Afrifa, General Robert Kotei, General Utuka and Colonel Roger Felli (a one-time Commissioner for External Affairs in Archeampong's regime) were similarly executed. Eight senior officers in all (three of them former Heads of State of Ghana) were executed on the orders of Ghana's Armed Forces Revolutionary Council.

I was not happy when these executions were carried out in Ghana by the Armed Forces Revolutionary Council in 1979. I attacked Jerry Rawlings and his colleagues of the Armed Forces Revolutionary Council for ordering the execution of the officers in an article published by one of Nigeria's Sunday newspapers. The article which was titled "Tragedy in Ghana" said *inter alia*:

> The more I try to forget the sad and tragic events in Ghana, the more I become unable to resist the urge of making my views known. I know Ghana too well. Since 1976 I have visited Ghana at least seven times now. As a convinced Nkrumaist, I have always taken very keen interests in Ghana's affairs.... It may be the mistake of some Africans to regard the Rawlings drama in Accra as a revolutionary action backed up with some ideological fire works. The Rawlings show has no link whatsoever with any radical revolutionary action. The coup was simply a coup of some confused trigger happy soldiers who had certain grievances against their superior officers. The talk by Jerry Rawlings of attempting a Mengistu type of revolutionary upsurge in Ghana at best could be dubbed the rantings of an opportunist.

If the revolutionary elements make the mistake in Ghana in ever embracing the murderous Rawlings group, it will surely be their last.

Ghana's present plight has portrayed the country in the words of Blair Thomson as a country that has cut off its own head. It appears that it may take Ghana a long time to recover from the curse put on her since the overthrow of progressive Kwame Nkrumah.

Progressive revolutionary forces in Africa must now start thinking seriously of what eventually happens to our great continent. Is our continent cursed? Are we now to start threading the path of insanity that many of the Latin American republics have been passing through since end of the second world war? Tragic events now happening in Africa daily must move us to do something fast...

Africa now looks for progressive leadership. For Africa to survive the challenges of the 80s, there must emerge now a highly effective leader whose operations and development strategies will completely destabilise all anti-Africa forces. Such a leader will be able to debunk the stupid assertion of the imperialist world that we in Africa are still unable to govern ourselves.

The Nkrumaists must disband the entire Ghana Army as presently constituted and go the whole length as Nyerere did in Tanzania in 1963... If the Nkrumaists do not do this and rush to take over power with an undisciplined army that becomes ready made tools for imperialism, Chile of Salvador Allende will be a child's play when viewed with the eventual result of such a foolish action in Ghana.

The whole world will continue to watch events in Ghana as the Rawlings drama continues.

The Armed Forces Revolutionary Council eventually handed over power to a democratically elected civilian government of the People's National Party (PNP) led by the late Alhaji Imoru Egala. On 24th September, 1979, Jerry Rawlings handed over power to President Hilla Limann at a colourful ceremony in Accra.

Many political observers of Ghana politics have said that but for the intervention of Jerry Rawlings and his colleagues of the Armed Forces Revolutionary Council, the Peoples' Front Party led by Victor Owusu would have been manipulated into power by the Akuffo government.

The third republic in Ghana was born on 24th September 1979 and it was an experiment that lasted only twenty-seven months.

At the handing over ceremony, ex-President Hilla Limman delivered the following memorable inaugural address before the Ghana Parliament:

> Never before since independence, have the demands of Government been greater, the tasks heavier and the fears, hopes and expectations higher than now.
>
> Abysmal economic chaos, awesome challenges and monumental responsibilities confront us in the face of measureless hope and ever-rising expectations.
>
> Founded out of a deep concern for the welfare of the people, my Government of the People's National Party shall not shirk its responsibility to them. We can not afford the luxury of failure.
>
> Our systems, beliefs and values, indeed our very existence as a nation are on trial. The need to re-awaken faith in ourselves as a people and in our ability to tackle and solve our problems has never therefore been greater than now. I believe that out of our present wreck we can build anew.
>
> Mine is a vision of Ghana in which the majority of our people shall be drastically cured so that, working selflessly together in unity, we shall serve mother Ghana. No effort shall be spared to cleanse our public life.
>
> You may think that I am promising the moon; well even the moon was reached and its rocks brought down to earth.
>
> But I am not promising the moon. What I am promising is a government that will work, a government that will be open and honest, modest yet vigorous; one that will wage a relentless war on poverty and corruption, indiscipline, inefficiency and dishonesty while upholding the rule of law.
>
> As we move into my administration, let me assure you and all

Ghanaians that, guided by the lessons drawn from the events since June 4, 1979, firm in my own commitment to open and clean government, based on participatory democracy at all levels, I shall not flinch from checking all forms of abuse and I hope I can count on the support of Honourable Members of Parliament. Together we all want a peaceful and stable atmosphere which will enable us to tackle our onerous responsibilities relentlessly without fear or favour.

Your Excellencies, Distinguished Guests, Ladies and Gentlemen, I wish finally to reiterate my appeal to all Ghanaians to join me in the national endeavour to salvage the honour and pride of our country. To this end, I pray for God's guidance and blessing to enable me to protect the most precious gift Ghanaians have given me – their confidence – which I accept in all humility and which I shall treasure with all my mind and all my strength only for as long as I retain their trust.

Hilla Limann was unable to retain the trust of Ghanaian citizens as his regime failed to honour all the promises he made to the people on 24th September, 1979. The PNP administration collapsed and the third republic was buried unceremoniously on Friday, 31st December 1981.

5
The Collapse of the Third Republic

Jerry John Rawlings is back in Ghana as the history of the tiny African republic now takes a decisive turn. Ghana, the country built by Kwame Nkrumah into a giant citadel of the African struggle against colonialism, is of extreme importance to Africa. It was there in Ghana that the first shots against colonialism were fired with the declaration of independence by Kwame Nkrumah on 6th March 1957: "The independence of Ghana is meaningless unless linked up with the total independence of the rest of Africa... At last the battle is over and beautiful Ghana is free for ever" declared the Osagyefo Kwame Nkrumah.

From 1957 to 24th February 1966, Ghana witnessed the era of a progressive administration under Nkrumah and the country was a pace setter for the rest of Africa. In the struggle for authentic African freedom from colonialism, Ghana took the pride of place. In Pan-African struggles, Nkrumah created an African country determined to lead the rest of Africa. Ghana became the capital of the African Revolution. Accra became the nursery of revolutionary African patriots who had been humiliated out of their respective countries by colonial interest and their lackeys. Ghana, the tiny Ghana, became the Mecca of progressive and radical opinion in Africa.

The Convention People's Party reputed to be the best organised party in Africa of those days, alongside the Action Group of Nigeria, dictated the pace of this wonderful era in Ghana. The CPP led by Nkrumah had its teething problems. True, the party had a hard core of revolutionary leaders like Nkrumah, Kojo Botsio, John Tettegah, Tawiah Adamafio and others; the party also had a great number of political dead-weights and arch reactionaries.

While Nkrumah was developing fast ideologically and was blazing a new ideological trail in Africa, several of his colleagues in the CPP leadership were empty-headed politicians who took delight only in sharing political offices in the country. It was these reactionaries that cleverly seized the mantle of leadership between 1963 and 1966 and thus neutralised Kwame Nkrumah from the genuine progressives of the party. With the seizure of the base of political power in the CPP by these reactionaries, it was thus easy for Tawiah Adamafio, the then energetic Information Minister, to be framed up as plotting to overthrow Kwame Nkrumah. He was accused of having planned the Kulungugu bomb attempt on the life of Nkrumah. He spent the rest of the days of Ghana's First Republic from 1963 to 1966 in prison. It was also easy for these arch lackeys of imperialism in Ghana to neutralise the radical trade unionists in Ghana and isolated them completely from Kwame Nkrumah. Thus by 1965, most of the energetic trade union leaders like Comrade Ofei Henaku and Kofi Ameko in Ghana had been sent abroad as ambassadors. John Tettegah the strongman of the Trades Union Congress was appointed a roving Minister for trade union matters with his base outside Accra. When the reactionary coup of Afrifa and Kotoka took place on 24th February 1966, there was no radical voice present to mobilise the people of

Ghana against the unfortunate coup.

The life of the CPP was terminated by the coup and no purge of the revisionists and party renegades was ever carried out. It had been said that Kwame Nkrumah was planning to return from Hanoi in 1966 to purge the party. Unfortunately, the purge never came and the evils of the CPP were then swept under the carpet. These evils surfaced when the Peoples National Party was formed and all the remnants of the CPP came together in the party. This is the major reason why Hilla Limann was toppled from power.

Hilla Limann, a former civil servant in Ghana's Foreign Service, inherited all the problems of the CPP. When in 1979, Ghana announced a return to civilian rule and permitted party formation, nearly all the members of Nkrumah's CPP came together in the People's National Party. The founder of the party was the late Imoru Egala from Northern Ghana who was ideologically miles apart from Kwame Nkrumah. The failure of Egala to win the party's presidential nomination as a result of the ban by the then Military Government led by the late General Akuffo, marked the beginning of the problems of the PNP. Imoru Egala got the first PNP Conference to ratify the nomination of his fellow tribesman Hilla Limann who was never in the CPP vanguard and who was even alleged to have been a hardened critic of Nkrumah. Hilla Limann, a stranger to CPP, won the presidential nomination and the PNP grudgingly accepted him, thereby postponing the evil day.

It is on record that some ideologically inclined Nkrumaists and who were members of the CPP refused to team up with the PNP on the grounds that the PNP could not be rightly regarded as a successor party to the CPP. Osei Poku, the radical editor of *Accra Evening News* refused to have anything to do with the party. He predicted a gloomy end for the party and labelled it an opportunist offshoot of the CPP. Johny Hansen, the revolutionary lawyer who in 1970 sold over two thousand pictures of Kwame Nkrumah at a rally in Kumasi and who was a principal actor in the anti-Union Government campaigns in the days of General Acheampong, formed his own party – PRP – which was registered by the electoral commission. Johny Hansen was later persuaded by well-meaning Nkrumaists to team up with the PNP when it was clear that the PFP of Victor Owusu, an offshoot of Busia's Progress Party, might win the elections.

The PNP won the 1979 elections on the CPP platform. Portraits of Kwame Nkrumah were carried at all the party's rallies and campaigns. The image of Kwame Nkrumah decisively won the election for PNP and Hilla Limann emerged as the first post military President of Ghana. Hilla Limann never found his feet in Government as he became a grand prisoner of Osu Castle under the control and authority of the opportunist renegades of the old CPP who had taken total control of the mantle of leadership in the PNP.

The PNP was only six months in Government when the contradictions inherent in the party started to surface. An attempt by radical forces in the party to appoint John Tettegah as the General Secretary of the PNP was resisted by the party renegades. Thus in the 1980 Kumasi Conference of the party, Hilla Limann staged a personal coup d'etat by seizing all party offices, and appointing a caretaker executive for the party when it became quite clear that John Tettegah would sweep the polls at the Conference. The Chairman of the party, Nana Okutwer Bekoe, who had been an ardent supporter of John Tettegah's bid for the post of General Secretary of the party compromised with Imoru Egala and Hilla Limann. The first open attempt by authentic Nkrumaists to inject some of their members into the leadership had failed.

The Nkrumaists left Kumasi Conference badly bruised but not defeated and routed. They regrouped and the aftermath of the regrouping was the Jerry John Rawlings New Year's eve show in Ghana. The John Tettegah loyalists who see John Tettegah as the soul and spirit of Kwame Nkrumah never pardoned the reactionary old guards of the CPP who were in control of the PNP party machinery. The PNP left the May 1980 Conference at Kumasi sharply divided into two ideological camps.

Unfortunately for Limann, he started taking bad advice from the discredited old guards. Against public opinion, he retired Jerry Rawlings from the Armed Forces and also retired the two

Commanders of the Ghana Army, appointed by the Rawlings Armed Forces Revolutionary Council. Captain Kojo Tsikata was placed under house arrest and an unprecedented security hunt was mounted against his person.

Hilla Limann started a dangerous policy of divide and rule. Major Poku Mensah and Major Boakye-Djan, two top members of Rawlings' Armed Forces Revolutionary Council, were encouraged to start a vicious campaign of calumny and hate against Rawlings overseas. The two officers were also financed back to Accra to address a world press conference against Rawlings. These were all attempts by Limann to de-emphasise the popularity of Jerrry John Rawlings in Ghana. It was a useless venture. The persecution of Rawlings got to such a crisis point that a revolutionary movement called the "June 4th Movement" was formed by revolutionary Ghanaian Youths. Rawlings was put at head of the movement.

By the time the June 4th Movement came into the political arena in Ghana, Rawlings' popularity had increased tremendously in the country. The attempts by the Limann administration to whip up tribal prejudices against the Ewes (the tribes of Rawlings, Kojo Tsikata and John Tettegah) failed and the die was then cast for the end of Limann's administration in Ghana.

The failure of the Kumasi Conference of the PNP led to the formation of the Kwame Nkrumah Revolutionary Guards led by Marxist John Hansen. The John Tettegah supporters also regrouped and linked up with the London based CPP group publishers of *The Dawn*. *The Dawn* never accepted Limann as an Nkrumaist throughout the period of his rule. It must be noted that *The Dawn* had warned Marxist forces in Ghana to treat the new Rawlings regime with care. This will be discussed in detail later.

It was these revolutionary groups within the PNP that took Limann and the PNP leadership to court when it became clear that some of the party's leaders were gunning for a total takeover of the party apparatus. As a result of the court action filed by one Addae Amoako who later compromised with the Limann administration, the Bolgatanga Conference of the PNP fixed for 13th December, 1981 in

Northern Ghana could not be held. It was the beginning of the final death rites of the party.

Limann appears the architect of his own downfall. He gambled and toyed with power. He allowed sycophants and opportunist renegades to take over his government. He won power on the image of Kwame Nkrumah but refused to be guided by the teachings of Nkrumaism. Hilla Limann had the will to succeed in Ghana but he unfortunately had no drive, no mission and no goal.

6
The Jerry Rawlings Factor

The Third Republic of Ghana is no more. It collapsed on New Year's eve, 1981. Hilla Limann had prepared the grounds well for the disaster that befell Ghana and his regime.

Hilla Limann brutalised and pestered the life of Jerry John in Ghana. The Jerry John Rawlings that took over the reins of government from late Lieutenant General Fred Akuffo on 4th June 1979 was a naive military officer who was thoroughly un-ideological and whose only success was based on the opposition of the Ghanaian people to the corruption of the then military rulers. However, the persecution and oppression mounted against Rawlings by the Limann administration completely changed him. The Rawlings we now have in Ghana is a different person. He is now ideological. He appears to be a radical socialist and an uncompromisingly committed fighter for the cause of the oppressed. He has seen neo-colonialism at play. He has been a victim of the rottenness of the capitalist apparatus in Ghana.

During 1981 he was the Co-ordinator General of at least four principal revolutionary movements in Ghana, the June 4 Movement, the Kwame Nkrumah Revolutionary Guards, the Militant Ghanaian Students and the C.P.P. group in London. Ghana's intelligence squad was after his blood and Rawlings had to address many press conferences to correct the lies peddled against his person.

It was Limann who transformed Jerry John Rawlings into a fire-eating socialist crusader and the history of Ghana may benefit from this accident of history. I was a great critic of Rawlings as mentioned in an earlier chapter when he seized power in 1979 and ordered the decimation of the lives of eight military officers in Ghana. It was my contention then that the military was not the instrument for the establishment of an authentic movement of the people. I was of the opinion that Rawlings and his group would only succeed in eliminating the military elite in power without bothering about changing the bogus socio-economic system that had produced their victims. Events later proved me right.

Rawlings suffered as a result of his ideological naivety and the result of the Rawlings dilemma for Ghana might change the entire political history of Ghana and return the country to the beautiful Nkrumah days of old.

The Rawlings of 1982 is completely different from the Rawlings that seized power on the emotional and sentimental waves of opposition to the then military bourgeoisie in Ghana in 1979.

Jerry John Rawlings was retired from the Ghana armed forces in 1979. His retirement was sequel to a national controversy that broke out over an alleged jail break which led to the forced freedom and disappearance of Captain Victor Okaikwe, Captain Emmanuel Koda, Sergeant Monney and Sergeant Quartey. A week before the Ussher Fort prison jail break, the Ghana Broadcasting Corporation had broadcast a statement credited to Jerry Rawlings demanding the immediate release of officers who had earlier been convicted by the

Armed Forces Revolutionary Council. Jerry John Rawlings was subsequently retired and the road to 31 December 1981 began. Rawlings refused to take part in the Ghana Council of States' meetings of which he was a member by virtue of being a former Head of State.

Not long after Rawlings' retirement, his wife was thrown out of her job in an Accra-based commercial firm the Union Trading Company. Mrs. Rawlings was never given any reason for her dismissal and the gulf between Limann and Rawlings deepened.

To make matters worse, those who had assisted Rawlings in the 4th June 1979 coup were turned against him. Major Boakye-Djan (who had been the spokesman of the Armed Forces Revolutionary Council) and Major Poku Mensah became agents provocateur of the Limann administration against Rawlings.

Captain Kojo Tsikata, a good friend of Jerry Rawlings was arrested by Limann and later declared a security risk. He was confined to his house and military intelligence mounted a twenty-four hour vigil on him. Captain Kojo Tsikata refused to be broken. He never denied his political association with Rawlings.

Then came a spate of malicious and false security reports against the person of Jerry Rawlings. He was accused by the Limann government of establishing training camps for the purpose of overthrowing the government. Many soldiers were sacked and many were sent to prison as a result of these false charges. Rawlings himself was arrested for sometime and later released. Limann, suspecting that Libya was fully supporting Rawlings, immediately broke diplomatic relations with Libya and ordered all the Libyan staff in Ghana to leave the country.

The final straw that broke the camel's back in the relationship between Limann and Rawlings was the humiliation handed down to Rawlings on his return from Libya. In September 1981, Rawlings was invited by Muammar Gaddafi to attend the September Libyan independence celebrations. At the end of the visit, Rawlings travelled via Cotonou, Republic of Benin. Mathieu Kerekou promptly gave him a befitting treatment as a former Head of State. The Ghana government, having learnt of the incident, immediately contacted the Togolese authorities. Immediately Rawlings was sighted in the Togolese territory, he was stopped and searched. The official escort and car from the Republic of Benin were sent back to Cotonou on the order of the Togolese authorities and Rawlings was questioned for a long time at the border. Rawlings had to travel back to Accra through the grace of a good samaritan, who having recognised him, stopped to give him a lift. Limann thus paved the way for his own downfall. Progressive opinion was mobilised against him and the fall came unexpectedly on 31st December, 1981.

Jerry Rawlings himself had predicted the fall of the Limann administration as far back as 4th June 1981 when he was addressing the June 4th Movement on the anniversary of the June 4 coup. He declared then:

> ...Ghana today is in the grip of a grave crisis. But the solutions cannot lie in a loss of confidence in own own people and abject submission to the economic domination of foreigners. That way we deny our very sovereignty and repudiate the hopes of our forebears who struggled to free us from the colonial yoke ...
> Those who have their ears turned towards the people will also know what value the people place on the June 4 day as an opening toward their realisation of those ideals. We end by recalling the words of John F. Kennedy many years ago: "Those who make a peaceful revolution impossible make a violent revolution inevitable".

In my book *Coups: Africa and the Barrack Revolts* I summed up the Ghana situation thus:

> The situation in Ghana now under the Peoples National Party government is also grave. The fear of a possible comeback of the army still haunts the civilian regime. All the appointees of the Rawlings government in the Armed Forces were compulsorily retired by the Hilla Limann Government. The Commander of the Army under the Armed Forces Revolutionary Council was

retired. Flight Lieutenant Jerry Rawlings himself was also retired.

Flight Lieutenant Jerry Rawlings who still resides in Ghana has been showing signs of being interested in active political life. His mass popularity continues to be a problem to the civilian administration.

In a special article I wrote for the *Sunday Sketch* on 2nd December 1979 on the Ghana situation, I concluded thus:

> Hilla Limann and the PNP must succeed. Nkrumaism must be fully rooted in Ghanaian society as a counter point to all the years of corruption and fascism in the country.
> Everything however depends on Hilla Limann and of course "J.J." Jerry John Rawlings. It is a million good luck to Ghana.

I have been proved conclusively right.

Hilla Limann failed to utilise the tremendous opportunities offered him by the mass popularity of Kwame Nkrumah in Ghana. Instead he chose the path of perfidy by spending and wasting precious time chasing the shadow. He was much more concerned with the security of himself in government and eventually ended up securing no one (not even himself). He pursued Rawlings until he succeeded in turning virtually every revolutionary Ghanaian citizen against his regime. Limann fell on New Year's eve 1981 and no one shed tears for his political demise. What a pity!

7
Corruption in High Places

One of the principal reasons why the Third Republic collapsed in Ghana was corruption. Corruption was rampant during the period of PNP rule in Ghana. The cedi fell to its lowest value in the Limann days. Despite this factor, a privileged minority experienced no shortage, no inconvenience throughout the period of Limann rule. The PNP in its economic policies, bent backwards to please multinational interests by encouraging liberalisation of trade to the detriment of the nation's economy. This was another major reason for the collapse of the regime.

It would be unfair for one to accuse Hilla Limann of being a corrupt leader. There is no evidence to accuse Hilla Limann of corruption, and there may never be any charge. He however presided over a very corrupt administration. To his credit Hilla Limann showed signs of being a determined ruler guided by national interests. However his civil service method (he was a former career diplomat) of dealing firmly with men and issues ruined his regime.

I was in Ghana in November 1981 and the corruption and confusion I saw in that country convinced me that if something fundamental was not done quickly to rescue Ghana, the future of the country was hanging in the balance. The situation was so bad that newpapers carried daily articles calling for a Messiah to redeem Ghana of her sins.

One such article in the Accra *Free Post* stated *inter alia:*

> All aspects of our national life are in a shambles, and Ghanaians are suffering even more than they did before. Food and commodity prices are higher than ever before. Shortages are more critical than before, and we continue to face a very grim future. While the government flounders about, weighed down by incompetence and corruption we are still faced with stagnation in our agricultural sector.

The article ended on this note:

> We must take the PNP away from those whose undemocratic unwillingness to permit it to adopt a truly grass root popular character, will surely ruin the party in much the same way as the CPP was destroyed.
>
> If we don't work towards these objectives there will be disaster; we will surely lose the confidence of the people. We will surely lose the next elections. We might even lose the third republic, and history will surely judge us harshly.

And the Third Republic in Ghana fell under the corruption and parochialism of the PNP policy makers.

Early in 1980, some PNP leaders started accusing each other of having secured importation licenses to order certain scarce essential commodities into Ghana. These accusations came into the open when the tussle for power between Nana Okutwer Bekoe and the father of the party, late Alhaji Imoru Egala, broke into the open. Nana

Okutwer Bekoe was accused of having been given an import license to bring in certain commodities into Ghana. The propriety of the offer was questioned within the party and Nana Okutwer Bekoe was forced to issue many rejoinders against the charge. It was, however, true that several PNP leaders who caught the ears of Hilla Limann were given import licenses to bring in the scarce essential commodities. The results of these illegal deals further impoverished the masses of the people of Ghana. Super markets were open in several parts of Ghana with the result that only the rich barons of the PNP had access to the very expensive markets they had created.

In March 1981, a member of the parliament of People's Front Party (PFP), Dr. T. K. Aboagye accused leaders of the PNP of corruption. He alleged that the PNP had established an account into which regional ministers of the party were required to pay 1 million Cedi (Ghana currency) every month. Beside a mere statement of denial by the People's National Party, there was no official reaction from the Hilla Limann government.

Two grave national scandals that rocked the Hilla Limann government in 1981 were the Thomas De la Rue and the Marino Chiavelli scandals. Late in November 1981, some PNP leaders were accused by certain parliamentarians of having got kick backs from Thomas De la Rue, a British Printing Company that specialises in the printing of bank notes. The company was accused of having paid ten percent kickbacks of £2.7 million to some leaders of the PNP. The controversy surrounding this scandal was still raging in Ghana by the time the Rawlings' New Year eve show occurred. Three officials of the People's National Party, Mr. Kofi Batsa, Chairman of the Publicity Committee of the party; Dr. Ivan Addae-Mensah, the General Secretary of the party; and Nana Okutwer Bekoe were accused of having received the kickbacks from the British company. All the leaders promptly denied the charges. The British company, Thomas De la Rue, also denied ever giving kickbacks to anyone in Ghana. The accusation reflected the general mistrust of Ghana's public officials by the time the coup took place.

One scandal that will continue to be remembered in the history of the Third Republic in Ghana is the Marino Chiavelli affair. His connection with Ghana dates back to the period of Busia's rule in the early seventies. Sometime in 1981 Marino Chiavelli filed a suit in a London High Court against two leaders of the PNP, Mr Kwasi Ofori and Mr Krobo Edusei. In the suit, Mr. Chiavelli who now resides in South Africa alleged that he had given a loan of 700,000 dollars to the People's National Party of Ghana on the 13th of October, 1979. Mr. Chiavelli claimed that the money was never repaid to him.

I took the opportunity of my visit to Ghana in November 1981 to investigate this accusation against some PNP leaders. I discovered from my investigations that the allegation of a Chiavelli connection with some PNP leaders was indeed true. My sources could not however confirm whether money changed hands between Chiavelli and certain PNP leaders.

It was confirmed to me that Marino Chiavelli did visit Ghana in 1979. Certain PNP leaders were said to have held a party for Mr. Chiavelli at the Palm Court Inn, a beach hotel in Accra built by the Kwame Nkrumah regime. My sources further informed me that Palm Court Inn Accra was taken over for two days by the PNP leaders that hosted the Chiavelli visit. It was alleged that Mr. Marino Chiavelli was offered the post of Ghana's Ambassador-at-Large in exchange for the money paid to certain PNP leaders.

The Chiavelli affair completely destroyed the credibility of the Limann administration. It was this factor that made a PNP socialist militant declare to me in Accra in November 1981, "We can no longer tolerate a government of the few, for the few and by the few. We will fight anyone who would throw up rigid elitist dictatorial obstacles to frustrate the attempt of the rank and file of the PNP to reclaim their power."

Limann was not able to arrest the growing corrupting tendencies of some of his colleagues. While he appeared to be a sober and intelligent ruler who no doubt genuinely wished to succeed, he was too weak to deal hard blows on the sycophants and careerist opportunists that discharged the obligations of power on his behalf. His Vice-President Dr. De Graft Johnson seemed more concerned with his cigarette pipe than with accepting the challenges of office.

Limann's friendship with Alhaji Shehu Shagari of Nigeria was of no assistance to Limann in checking corruption in his administration as Nigeria was experiencing the same situation under the leadership of Shehu Shagari and the National Party of Nigeria. Lies were told by some PNP leaders against Chief Obafemi Awolowo and UPN leaders in order to gain the favour of Alhaji Shehu Shagari and support from a more economically buoyant neighbour. The UPN was accused of having master-minded the killings of some Ghanaian citizens in Nigeria by Ekow Daniels, a one time Minister of Hilla Limann. The Unity Party of Nigeria was forced to despatch a two man delegation led by Alhaji Abdulkadir Young-Sidi to Ghana to debunk and refute the unsubstantiated lies. Ekow Daniels was later dismissed from office in September 1981 after making a malicious allegation against Hilla Limann himself. It was too late before Limann discovered the character of such charlatans in his government.

Hilla Limann is now an ex-Head of State of Ghana. He had every opportunity to succeed in Ghana but frittered everything away on the altars of political immaturity, ambivalence and indecision. He permitted the reign of sycophants and business tycoons and so sentenced his regime to an abrupt end. The end came on a New Year's eve.

Despite his seeming good intentions, the Limann administration failed in practically everything it tried to do. When the time of the collapse came, the same evil forces that contributed to the fall of Nkrumah in 1966 again vanished into thin air. Krobo Edusei was the first to denounce the Limann PNP regime while giving evidence in a probe ordered by the Provisional National Defence Council. Hilla Limann attempted to rule Ghana by prostituting the progressive ideas and programmes of Osagyefo Kwame Nkrumah. He has now gone the way of all imposters. The search for genuine Nkrumaists in Ghana continues. Can Rawlings really revive the Nkrumah's days of old in Ghana? It is to the future that Ghana must now look.

8
Proclamation of the Ghana Revolution

Having given the various factors that led to the fall of Ghana's Third Republic, it is important that the events of the Ghana coup of 31st December 1981 be recorded for posterity. During my visit to Accra in April 1982, I tried as much as possible to put together the events of the coup. I nosed around for news and it is my contention that the coup has unique lessons for most of the Third World.

The Hilla Limann PNP administration used all the resources at its call to avert a coup in Ghana. The Ghana intelligence squad was strengthened and most of its officers were sent overseas for further training. The Ghana Air Force was decentralised and many of its units were posted to obscure centres in Ghana in order to prevent a sudden Rawlings takeover of the Air Force for an attempt on the administration. The security council headed by ex-President Hilla

Limann met often to review the security situation in Ghana. Beautiful Ghana women who were members of Ghana's intelligence squad were posted to take permanent residence in Ghana's big hotels. Their mission was to report on questionable characters that might be using night life to plan subversive activities against the government of Ghana. I was privileged to have met one of these young women at the Penta Hotel, Accra in 1980 who later confessed her mission to me and further informed me that Ghana had survived three attempted coup d'etat as of that time. Despite all the precautionary steps taken by the Limann government to prevent a coup d'etat, the regime collapsed on 31st December, 1981.

At the time Jerry Rawlings and his fellow revolutionaries struck against the Limann administration, it was evident that the PNP administration had outlived its usefulness to the people of Ghana. Civilians were even plotting to over-throw the government through constitutional means. The coup climate was so serious in Ghana that by 24th December 1981, a hurried security council meeting was called at the instance of both the Defence Minister Riley Poku and Minister for Special Duties (Security) Dr. Nabilla with President Hilla Limann presiding. The Minister for Defence was said to have submitted a detailed security report to the council of a possible coup attempt on the administration. President Hilla Limann was said to have requested the Security Council to postpone discussions on the matter till after the Christmas and New Year celebrations. The meeting broke up without resolutions on the matter.

On 26th December (Boxing Day) Jerry Rawlings and some soldiers were invited by Ghana Security led by Colonel Annor Odjija (a fellow Somanya-Ade tribesman with Kofi Botsia) for questioning. They were interrogated at the Burma Camp. Jerry was told at the questioning that the authorities had received information of a coup being planned by some soldiers to restore Jerry Rawlings to power. Jerry was said to have denied categorically any knowledge of such an affair. Some people close to Jerry informed me that it was after he (Jerry Rawlings) returned from Burma Camp that he made up his mind to support any move that might be made to terminate the Hilla

Limann government.

On 30th December 1981, President Hilla Limann, Vice President Dr. De Graft Johnson and several ministers attended the end of year party of soldiers at the Burma Camp. Close confidants of Hilla Limann later advised him to leave the party for security reasons but had hardly reached his residence when the coup broke out.

The coup was started by eight soldiers who took control of four armoured vehicles and went directly to the house of the Commander of the Recce squadron. The Commander escaped but the eight coup plotters seized total control of the Recce. Rawlings was immediately brought into the coup and it was he who later mobilised the Ghana Air Force behind the coup.

The soldiers at Burma Camp, having known that Jerry Rawlings was involved in the coup, gave immediate support and fought on the side of the coup makers to oust the Limann administration.

Immediately sporadic shooting was heard in Accra, Riley Poku, the Minister for Defence, and Dr. Nabilla, the Minister for Special Duties (Security) started to make counter moves to crush the coup. A fake signal was sent to certain army units outside Accra that Ghana was being invaded from outside. The army unit at Takoradi responded to the signal and marched down to Accra to resist a fake invasion led by Colonel Agbama. This explained the initial resistance that the coup met. The soldiers quickly laid down their arms when it became clear to them that there had been no invasion and that Jerry Rawlings was in charge of the situation. Colonel Agbama was immediately arrested.

The shootings which started on the night of 30th December 1981 moved to the early hours of 31st December. At about 11.00am Jerry Rawlings and his fellow coup executors marched in four armoured vehicles with about six trucks full of soldiers to the Ghana Broadcasting House behind Army headquarters at the Redemption Circle, Accra to make a broadcast to the people of Ghana. They were overwhelmed with civilian support.

Hilla Limann's Chief of Defence Staff, Air Vice Marshall Odartey Barnor, fled in an armoured vehicle which was later found abandoned. The head of Ghana's intelligence squad, Colonel Annor Odjija, and the Commander of Ghana's Second Infantry, Brigade Colonel Ofosu Appiah, also fled into exile.

Many PNP officials who were involved in the last minute attempt to crush the coup disappeared into thin air immediately it became clear to them that their regime had been removed. One of the advisers of Hilla Limann, Owusu-Afriye, made for the border escaping to Ivory Coast.

Corporal Azambiya and Corporal Tetteh, popularly known as "C.C.", and Sergeant Alolga Akatapore (a second year student of economics at the University of Cape Coast who was on holidays at the time of the coup) participated actively in the coup.

The coup however had its casualties. Fifteen soldiers including four officers were killed in the military operations.

President Hilla Limann was arrested about the third day of the coup along with two of his security guards while trying to cross the Ghana border. He is now held in detention at the Presidential lodge at Akosombo. Vice-President De Graft Johnson was also arrested and detained.

By first of January 1982, it was all over. A provisional national defence council was established to rule Ghana.

There were immediate reactions to the Ghana coup from all parts of the world. The Nigerian Federal Government was immediately hostile to the Rawlings regime and oil supplies to Ghana were cut off. Many of the western European countries were also hostile to the Rawlings coup. However, Ghanaians were quick to organise demonstrations in defence of the coup. Both the American embassy and the Nigerian High Commission in Accra were attacked by the demonstrating Ghanaian citizens. The Unity Party of Nigeria led by one of Africa's foremost leaders of all time, Chief Obafemi Awolowo, did not waste time in issuing a press release to the world on the Ghana situation.

The press release said *inter alia*:

The collapse of the Third Republic in Ghana offers Africa and Africans some moments of sober reflection. The events cannot but produce sadness and sorrow, more so when a civilian administration in Ghana that gave hope to the toiling masses there had to collapse within thirty months of its existence to the country's armed forces.

It is said that media houses in Nigeria controlled by the National Party of Nigeria have considerably played down the news of events in Ghana. The NTA Channel 10 Lagos did not offer Nigerians the opportunity of hearing about the events in Ghana. Instead the television station chose to be criminally quiet without regard to the professional ethics which enjoin journalists to regard facts as being sacred. The few new reports broadcast on the television station have been coloured with prejudice and bias. this situation does not speak well of the role of a responsible media house in a democratic setting.

The collapse of Hilla Limann's administration in Ghana should not be dismissed as one of the frequent military eruptions in Africa. The ramifications of the event certainly go beyond the borders of Ghana. It is bound to affect the new democratic climate now being planted in Africa.

Parliament has been dissolved, Hilla Limann's administration has been sacked, politicians are now being arrested while about ten people were reported killed during the coup action. Ghana has now entered another era of military rule.

We of the Unity Party of Nigeria consider the people of Ghana as the best judges of the situation. They are the people who are directly affected by the events. We are however mindful of the fact that the collapse of Ghana's Third Republic is a general trial of civilian politicians in Africa.

Politicians are elected to serve the people. They are supposed to be the guiding angels of democratic principles and ideals. Politicians are not to feather their own nests and criminally neglect the interests of the people they are supposed to serve. Corruption, acts of personal aggrandizement, ethnic chauvinism and unnecessary fratricidal struggles created by renegade politicians to divert the attention of the people from meaningful programmes have been the major reasons for the termination of many a civilian regime in Africa. The root causes of the recent Ghana affair cannot be far from all these.

The return of Ghana and Nigeria to normal democratic regimes in 1979 certainly gave a new spirit and hope to many patriots in Africa. With the collapse of the Limann administration in Ghana, many will now doubt have started to quiver about the future of democracy in Africa. This is where we direct the attention of all the current political actors in Nigeria.

Nigeria is always referred to as the giant of Africa (or so we regard ourselves). We, the political actors in Nigeria, must therefore strive by our behaviour and conduct to make the civilian experiment succeed. We must put the national interests above the narrow and mad pursuits of ill-gotten individual wealth and property accumulation. We must strive to give to the people of this country a government that genuinely believes in *people* and their overall welfare.

We of the Unity Party of Nigeria sympathise with the innocent and ordinary citizens of Ghana who are now bearing the brunt of the acts of omission and commission of the Hilla Limann administration.

If we are sure of anything, it is that there can never be any substitute in Africa for democracy as a form of government. We of the Unity Party of Nigeria therefore call on retired Flight Lieutenant Jerry Rawlings to immediately start the process of allowing the masses of the Ghanaian people who are in the majority to decide soonest how best they will wish to be governed.

We call on Jerry Rawlings and the Provisional National Defence Council to initiate without delay a programme for the return to normal democratic rule. Any further delay may sentence Ghana to a history of anarchy and disaster. But God forbid.

We of the Unity Party of Nigeria also call on Jerry John Rawlings and the Provisional National Defence Council not to allow their holy war on corruption to involve the sadistic termination of innocent human lives. Africa has witnessed unnecessary horrendous killings and it is our belief that any recourse to senseless shedding of human blood in Ghana will only complicate the problems of the country and produce no results.

We of the Unity Party of Nigeria also call for an urgent understanding of the economic problems of Ghana by countries in Africa that have the means to help. Ghanaians are no beggars and they have a great history that they can always be very proud of (Nkrumah's Ghana — the shining light of Africa). It is our contention however that ECOWAS can only be meaningful if Nigeria and Ivory Coast, two seeming affluent members of the Community, can give meaningful understanding to the economic problems of Ghana and give a helping hand. It is clear to us that Ghana will continue to live under political uncertainty for as long as their economy continues to be in a shambles. Democratic habits can only be nurtured in societies where stability (political, economic and social) reigns supreme. Instability in any African country must necessarily produce repercussions in others. African politicians must learn from the Ghana experience. Hilla Limann might have meant well but certainly he presided over an administration whose interests ran parallel and counter to the interests of the masses of the people in Ghana.

African politicians must learn that corruption in whatever guise does not pay. What preserves a society and makes stability to endure is the firm and unrelenting commitment of those given the mantle of leadership and authority to the genuine yearnings and aspirations of the people they govern.

We appeal to Jerry John Rawlings and the Provisional National Defence Council to allow the people of Ghana have the final say on their own matters. A military solution will only produce shock results and merely scratch the surface. It can never produce the lasting solutions.

80 The Ghana Revolution

The Ghana revolution proclaimed after the coup by Jerry John Rawlings will have to be judged by the last sentence of the Unity Party of Nigeria release. This is examined in the last chapter of this book.

9
Dialogue with the Revolutionaries

I was invited by the Rawlings government to visit Ghana and observe the one hundred days of the new experiment in Ghana. I arrived in Ghana on the eve of the celebrations marking the tenth anniversary of the death of Kwame Nkrumah and I took the opportunity of my visit to exchange ideas with some of the revolutionaries of the Provisional National Defence Council. I asked searching questions on the progress of the Revolution and their general assessment. I now share their views with all those who may come into contact with this book.

An Interview with John Hansen (PNDC Secretary for the Interior)
John Hansen was of the view that the fall of the PNP had given opportunity for genuine Nkrumaists to participate in government and to put across the views of Kwame Nkrumah himself. When asked

to comment on his estimation of Rawlings and socialism, John Hansen, a rather small statured, socialist firebrand replied:

> There is no danger for the socialist Nkrumaists in Ghana. The Rawlings of 1979 is quite different from the Rawlings of 1982. I believe the experiences of Lieutenant J. J. Rawlings between 24th September 1979 and 31st December 1981 were enough lessons for him. His pronouncements since the 31st December coup have been more indicative of a recognition of the socialist ideological base which you consider to have been lacking in the 4th June 1979 coup.
>
> There is no danger for progressive forces in the government of the PNDC. There has never been a one hundred percent purity in struggle.

Asked to comment on soldiers and mass struggle with particular reference to the fact that soldiers trained in imperialist training camps tend to be neo-colonial in character and hence counter revolutionary, John Hansen replied:

> I can not claim to speak for a large number of soldiers who are supporters of Rawlings. There is clear evidence that all the soldiers who support Rawlings understand the ideological base of the 31st December revolution. As long as the revolution is a reflection of the struggles in Ghana, the soldiers will certainly continue to support the progressive policies and programmes of Jerry Rawlings. If you are basically anti elitist, anti petit-bourgeois, it is not difficult to communicate with the masses of the people including the soldiers as well. All Ghanaians are learning as the revolution continues to progress.

I put it to him that from my observations of the trend in Ghana politics, I deduced that there was alienation between the younger and older generations. John did not agree. His reply was:

> I do not believe there is alienation between the younger and the older generations. There is however some degree of alienation between the revolutionary younger generation and the

conservative status quo orientated older generation. There is more ideological clarity and commitment on the part of the younger generation than the older one.

I also put it to him that many of the PNP members who had fled into exile had accused Rawlings of promoting an Ewe inspired tribal coup. John Hansen was very unhappy at this charge. He told me point blank:

> The charge of tribalism is errant nonsense. This is not true. I can assure you there is no tribal element in the popular revolution that swept off the PNP administration. This is a revolution which involves all the people of Ghana including the Ewes, the Gas, the Akans, the Hausas and all. It is a revolution which all the oppressed and over-exploited people of Ghana understand. The basis of our people's support for the revolution is borne out of our experiences of exploitation and injustice. There is no tribal demarcation for injustice and exploitation. All exploited people share the same experiences no matter their tribes of origin which certainly is immaterial to the principal cause of their sufferings and dehumanisation.

It was exciting talking to John Hansen, who of all the members of the PNDC, had been in the Ghanaian struggle longest. He was a radical youth activist of Nkrumah's Convention People's Party. When the coup of 24th February 1966 came, John Hansen went into exile in Tanzania, and returned in 1969 to lead massive opposition to the reactionary government of Professor Kofi Busia. He was also a principal actor in the anti Union Government proposals of the late General Ignatius Kutu Acheampong. When it became apparent that the PNP had degenerated as an Nkrumaist-socialist party, John Hansen cleverly withdrew to form the radical Kwame Nkrumah Revolutionary Guards — one of the militant organisations now supporting the revolution in Ghana.

An Interview with Ama Atta Aidoo (PNDC Secretary for Education)
I also spoke extensively with Ama Atta Aidoo, the woman stormy

petrel of the revolution in charge of education. The interview with her was quite charged but interesting. Ama Atta Aidoo is a respected Ghanaian intellectual and has written several books on English. She was a lecturer at the University of Cape Coast at the time of the 31st December coup. Her socialist views are very much respected in Ghana. She was also a principal combatant in the struggles of the people of Ghana against the Union Government proposals and General Ignatius Acheampong, giving moral and unqualified support to the students in their opposition and struggle against Acheampong's Unigovernment.

Asked to comment on the composition of the PNDC which appeared an all comers affairs, Ama Atta Aidoo said:

> At the beginning of a revolutionary process, it may be necessary to co-opt and seek help form all sorts of forces who may not be identified as revolutionaries. The composition can only be reasonably determined by outside observers. It may not be historically and socially possible to have everybody who is in vanguard positions bringing in revolutionary philosophy. What is important for now is the consolidation of the national democratic revolution.
>
> In China, it was not until it became absolutely possible to launch a socialist revolution that the communist party of China could declare to the world their intentions. We have the intention in the PNDC to organise along revolutionary lines. We rely on our people and well-wishers to always observe us and call us regularly to order whenever they believe mistakes are being committed. What is happening in Ghana is a people's movement.

When I put it to her that soldiers, by virtue of their imperialist training and orientation have always betrayed popular revolutions, Ama Atta Aidoo was quick to reply:

> We hope it will not happen here. If the forces within the peoples' army in Ghana see a need for revolution then for once it is

possible that the pattern will be broken. History is a dynamic element. It is quite possible for new patterns to be initiated all the time. Let us hope that what is happening here is setting into motion new political patterns and the army can continue to see itself as an ally for the initiation of revolutionary policies rather than an enemy of revolutionary forces.

Asked to comment on the place and role of Ghanaian women in the new revolution, Ama said:

This is one of the important anomalies we are confronting in this era. Whereas the PNDC is committed to the people of Ghana to streamline production and distribution, it has therefore had to take some measures against people in commerce.

We have initiated educational programmes like symposia and rallies to educate women involved in trade as against what their contributions to revolution should be. We have called for their maximum co-operation. We are telling them of other areas where women's energies can be better utilised.

The problem of women mercantilists is only in the urban centres. In the rural areas, women are involved in agricultural production. Women have been underdogs in the system. This is why they have fallen into petty trade to the point that other meaningful avenues of trade have been closed to them. It is the duty of the present revolutionary process to take the role of women in society very seriously. We cannot give ready made answers to the problems of women but they are very much in view.

When asked what she would wish for herself in the future, Ama Atta Aidoo replied jocularly:

If I have any personal ambitions, it is that at some point I will be able to return to the writer Ama Atta Aidoo full time.

A writer can function optimally not only in terms of the contribution he/she makes to radical, political and social processes but also by maintaining the will to produce as a writer works that will continue to guide humanity to progress.

My wanting to return to my real self in future does not mean opting out entirely from the political process. My continued association with the political process depends on the people of Ghana.

An Interview with Ato Austin, (Secretary for Information)
Ato Austin the energetic and radical socialist secretary for information, was the last of the Ghana revolutionaries that I spoke to. Ato Austin is considered the chief spokesman of the Jerry Rawlings regime in Ghana. A young man of about thirty-four years, Ato Austin was dismissed as Secretary of the Youth wing of the People's National Party for his radical views and his rather harsh criticisms of PNP's opportunist ideological stance. A lawyer-chemist by profession, Ato Austin was said to have shunned an appointment with the United Nations to face the task of reconstructing the entire Ghana's socio-political life. His views were forthright. His demeanour pleasant and his eloquence unparalleled. As he spoke frankly to me, my mind simply prayed that Rawlings does not in future turn against him with the aim of completely silencing him. That has always been the fate and fortune of radical socialist forces who throw their intellect at the disposal of soldiers who masquerade as nationalists and paper revolutionaries. It is too early to determine what will be Jerry Rawlings' eventual ideological commitment. If Jerry Rawlings makes a roundabout turn in future (but God forbid) then the corpse of a dedicated revolutionary like Ato Austen may be picked on a street of Accra. It is important to document for posterity the full interview I had with this young dedicated socialist crusader.

Q: Don't you think the Ghana revolution is a mere paper revolution?

Ato: I will disagree with this conclusion. In the first stage of the revolution, the masses are often carried to undertake a lot of spontaneous action. This often times is an immediate reaction to the grave problems facing them. The task of the revolution is to sustain this enthusiasm and channel it to realisable goals.

The initial euphoria is a reflection of a new relief from

oppression and exploitation. It is the same force that has to be used to attack the foundations of structures which created the oppressive regimes of the past.

In the agricultural as well as the economic sectors, spontaneous participation of the people has exposed the inability of past structures to deal with the problems of the people.

The movement of the students, workers and soldiers to the rural areas to help with agriculture has re-awakened the interest of the people. It has made the people realise that the old system can not just continue. The people now know that they must help themselves.

The revolution has identified the basic economic problems of Ghana. There is no doubt that Ghana's economic relationship with external trading partners, control of foreign capital and the economic structure were all colonial creations. These are things that must be dismantled. No one can however do it abruptly; hence one may court disaster.

One of the main weapons to be used to achieve this is the revolutionary enthusiasm of the people. We will strive to break the neo-colonial arrangements once and for all and attempt to recreate new avenues of nationalist feeling in the people. The People's National Party bent over backwards to please international finance capital. This culminated in their failure.

The PNP reinforced the neo-colonial relationship. We want to create a national economy — an economy that will be independent and self-reliant. We are doing this using the new awareness and support base of the people. The popular participation of the people of Ghana will aide us in this struggle. Ours therefore is no newspaper revolution.

Q: Do you think the soldiers agree with your ideological analysis of Ghana's situation?

Ato: I believe the soldiers agree. The ordinary soldiers share the same aspirations with the masses of the people. June 4, 1979 represented the identification of the soldiers to the feelings and aspirations of Ghana people. The ordinary soldiers of the Ghana Army rose against an officer corps that was extremely anti the people and that was also an instrument of class exploitation and oppression. The renegade senior officer corps of the Ghana Army just stepped into the shoes of the colonial masters.

The coup of 4th June 1979 showed the similarity of interests between the broad section of the military and the masses of the people. That action represents a major breakthrough for the people of Ghana in that the Ghana Armed forces broke their ties with the decadent past and allied with the people. The 31st December revolution merely went many steps forward on the gains of 4th June 1979.

The battle of consolidating power is taking place not only on the civilian front but also within the military. The two sides (civilian and military) are performing the same revolutionary roles. The power which used to be in the hands of the exploiters will never again be used to oppress and suppress the masses. The soldiers and the masses have broken their chains of oppression. It is doubtful whether they will want to be oppressed again.

Q: Don't you think there is clear alienation now between the younger and the older generation? If you agree with this analysis, won't you consider it dangerous to the revolution?

Ato: Over the last ten years, youths in Ghana have had complete disillusionment with the activities of the ruling classes. The youths as a whole have not been happy with the activities of the older generation. The youths see themselves as having not contributed to the problems now facing the country.

Out of these terrible problems, have arisen certain groups committed to the interests and rights of the common people of Ghana. What is happening now in Ghana is an expression of the wide gulf growing between the youths and the conservative older generation. There can be no danger to the revolution for as long as the revolution does not compromise its programmes and policies.

Q: What about the problem of bureaucracy? How do you safeguard the revolution with the presence of the kind of bureaucracy that has destroyed many a regime in Ghana?

Ato: Contemporary Marxist theory makes it clear that you can not use an old state machinery to effect a new change. Right from the word go, the revolution has attempted to make a total break with the past.

The structure of the PNDC is fundamentally different from the past. We have changed the title "Minister" to "Secretary" thereby de-emphasising the neo-colonial character of such a title. We have created a relationship between the PNDC and the PNDC Secretaries who run the ministries. We are seriously attempting to democratise the system. There is new direct communication between the Ministries and the PNDC.

We are also trying to revolutionise the institutions that deal with structure. Virtually all the institutions of government are undertaking structural changes because we realise that if we merely change the personalities at the head of these institutions without restructuring the institutions themselves, we will not be able to move forward. There is now a clear way in which the base now has a direct link and access to the top. We believe these steps will help us tackle the problem of bureaucracy.

Q: Do you forsee the future showdown between Jerry Rawlings and the socialist forces now serving this regime?

Ato: Rawlings does not operate alone. The main body of the Armed Forces are committed Marxists. Ghana was lucky in the sense that from about 1972, the Universities went into a period of Marxist education. We formed study groups in all the universities and consequently deepened our study of Marxism. The influence of the Marxists within the PNDC is quite strong.

Rawlings himself has moved a great deal from his nationalist position. He has a clear understanding of imperialism which ignites the first phase of any struggle. Fidel Castro moved along the same lines.

There are certainly dangers in the way of all revolutionary regimes. All Marxist forces must mobilise and be vigilant. If we leave Rawlings alone in the struggle we will all pay for the foolishness.

The use of violence or force as a midwife for any social revolution is a delicate balance of one's own understanding of historical situation. Rawlings is prepared and determined to prevent the emergence of violence in that respect. He has impressed upon all the need for reorientation and understanding as opposed to the use of violence and force.

For a revolution to assume either a fascist or repressive character depends largely on the attitude of the people. The People's defence committees will also help in preventing the rise of fascists in Ghana. All the moves we are trying to make are to put power squarely in the hands of the people. This will prevent the emergence of the kind of situation you are afraid may become the eventual fate of the Ghana Revolution.

Q: What is the attitude of the Ghana Revolution to external relations?

Ato: We are going to heighten the need for economic independence of African and Third World countries. We shall spell out in detail the international character of imperialism.

Our foreign policy will be dictated by the jealous protection of our national interests. Our national interests must be based on our assessment and understanding of neo-colonialism.

We shall pursue vigorous development of relationships with Third World countries.

We see the foreign policy of Kwame Nkrumah as being very positive, dynamic and progressive. We shall make efforts to heighten it because we believe that the effective prosecution of the African Revolution is crucial to the survival of Ghana.

We shall equally establish diplomatic relations with all

progressive countries of the world. Ghana has already established one with Cuba.

Ghana will strive to recreate the beautiful Nkrumah's Ghana of old. This is the mission and goal of our foreign policy.

It was indeed interesting talking to Ato Austin who is regarded as the most senior civilian aide of Jerry Rawlings. The future will certainly tell whether his ideological analysis of the Rawlings regime will stand the test of time.

10
The Ghana Revolution — An Evaluation

On the morning of the coup of 31st December 1981, Jerry Rawlings opened his broadcast to all Ghanaians thus:

> Fellow Ghanaians, as you will notice, we are not playing the national anthem. In other words, this is not a coup. I ask for nothing else than a revolution — something that will transform the social and economic order of this country. The military is not in to take over. We simply want to be a part of the decision making process in this country. As a result of this, we are reinstating Brigadier Quainoo as the Army Commander and the former Chief of Staff Brigadier Nunoo Mensah.

Those words of Jerry Rawlings opened a new page and chapter in Ghana's political history. A revolution was formally declared and the people of Ghana went into unprecedented rejoicing over the whole affair. I chose the time I visited Ghana to assess the revolution and attest at first hand to its progress.

I was invited by the Jerry Rawlings Government to visit Ghana after the one hundred days of the revolution. I was unable to accept the invitation then as a result of heavy commitments to other political matters in Nigeria but I honoured the invitation to Ghana on the eve of "May-day". It was indeed a unique experience.

I was privileged to be at a workers' rally where Ato Austen, the PNDC Secretary for Information was trying to educate some members of the People's Defence Committees as to the goals of the Revolution. His powerful address was very inspiring and the workers responded positively at every stage to Ato's words of inspiration. He said *inter alia*:

> Ghana is in a revolutionary era. The Peoples Defence Committee is an expression of the people to rediscover themselves. It is the only means by which we can get the people organised and mobilised.
>
> There will be period of crisis. Ghana will have to go through all the stages of crisis so that our progress can be lasting. As far as the media is concerned, we will ensure that positive contributions of the PDCs to the revolution are highlighted.
>
> During this era there will be periods of shortages and the enemy will like to use the situation against the revolution. This era means a lot of hardship for many of us. The revolution requires sacrifices. We must give them in the interest of our country and ourselves.
>
> The Peoples Defence Committees must discover the talents of the ordinary workers and recognise efficiency. We must make this country work. This is the challenge for us all.

The workers were charged by the powerful oratory of Ato Austen. As he concluded with the slogan of the Ghana revolution by saying "PEOPLE", the workers roared back in reply "REVOLUTION". The slogan of the Ghana revolution put together is "PEOPLE —

REVOLUTION". It is exactly like the slogan of the socialist experiment in Kerekou's Benin Republic, "EWUSU DANDAN" meaning "power to the people".

Ghana no doubt is in a revolutionary fervour. It would be incorrect, however, to state that there are no problems. Enemies of the revolution who are now in exile have already announced the formation of a Save Democracy Movement. The movement is led by top members of the banned People's National Party. The movement has its offices in London and Lagos. The anti Rawlings front has also succeeded in recruiting to its ranks all the colleagues of Rawlings in the Armed Forces Revolutionary Council who have severed relationship and connections with him since the past 1979 events. It would be unwise for Rawlings to write off this opposition.

There is no doubt that the Ghana people support the Rawlings revolution for as long as it continues to meet with their aspirations but there are fears being expressed by patriots that the revolution might degenerate into fascism, eventually collecting casualties from among its children. Many of the principal functionaries of the PNDC that I spoke to in Ghana dismissed this charge but experiences of other countries in Africa have shown that the eventual result of military coups that profess initially to be revolutionary is repression of democratic forces and mass murders. Liberia is a typical example of this situation. The coup of Master Sergeant Kanyan Doe in Liberia was heralded a revolution by all the revolutionary forces in Liberia. The radical Movement for Justice in Africa (MOJA) led by Dr. Togbah Tipoteh and the socialist People's Popular Party led by Bacchus Mathews declared their total and absolute support for the revolution. The revolution finally converged on the doors of the progressive forces in Liberia claiming its own casualties from them.

It is easy to dismiss the possible existence of this kind of situation in Ghana in view of the style of Rawlings now which is marked departure from the sadistic style the Armed Forces Revolutionary Council adopted for its operations in post June 1979 Ghana. Jerry Rawlings is now busy attempting to change the socio-political fabric of the Ghana nation. The character of a progressive revolution is judged by the social tasks it performs in society and by the revolutionary forces that participate in it. The Ghana revolution adequately meets these requirements.

There are structural changes observable in the revolutionary Ghana of Jerry Rawlings now. KALABULE has been driven underground but not eradicated. Government officials of the revolution even participate in the underground operations of the KALABULE, which is Ghana's name for illegal foreign exchange market. The touts at the Kotoka International Airport and other strategic locations have disappeared. There is enthusiasm in the faces of all Ghanaians. But there is equally fear written on some faces. The younger generation is bubbling with revolutionary fervour. They are the moving spirit and dynamo of the revolution but there is despair and frustration written in the faces of the older generation. This is a major disaster area for the revolution.

At a symposium organised to honour the 10th anniversary of Kwame Nkrumah's death at the Kwame Nkrumah Conference Centre on Friday, 30th April 1982, Dr. P. B. Baffour, a retired civil servant in Ghana, summarised the present mood of the older generation in Ghana thus: "Do not keep the revolution to yourselves alone. Involve all sectors of the Ghana nation." The message was well delivered and it was also well taken by all those present.

The students have been the greatest supporters of the revolution. They were, at one time prepared to close down their studies in the interests of the revolution. They went with other volunteers to evacuate abandoned cocoa bags to the Tema Harbour for transportation abroad. Many of these cocoa bags were evacuated from Ghana's hinterland to Accra. It was later discovered that the cocoa could not be shipped abroad because it had not been refined. Such is the revolutionary fervour and enthusiasm of the youths and students in the new Ghana of Jerry Rawlings.

There are however problems facing the revolution. Apart from the food problem which has remained largely unsolved, there are problems which, if allowed to grow, may cause a serious setback to the revolution. There is a general feeling among some progressive organisations in Ghana that their help is not needed. The African Youth Command the Kwame Nkrumah Revolutionary Guards believe that their organisations are being relegated to the background by the boys of the June 4 Movement who are mostly students. I was told in Accra that constant attempts are being made by some of the members of he June 4 Movement (an organisation that took its revolutionary name from the 4th June, 1979 military coup) to isolate other progressive organisations from the new experiment. If the trend continues, forces that should be permanent allies of the Revolution may be forced to adopt a wait and see posture which will certainly be dangerous for the Revolution and the revolutionary forces themselves. It must be stated, however, that Jerry Rawlings appears to understand this problem and has cleverly maintained the delicate balance between all the forces participating in the revolution.

Another problem facing the Revolution is the fact that the ideological character of it is not known. The supreme body of the ruling Provisional National Defence Council has refused to spell out in official terms the ideological character of the Ghana Revolution. At a London press briefing in March 1982, a spokesman of the PNDC described the Ghana Revolution as a continuation of the struggle for freedom and justice whose first peak had been nominal political independence in 1957. Jerry Rawlings himself was said to have declared that Ghana has never had anything to show for political independence. It was his contention that Ghanaian independence of 1957 was a mere paper and flag independence. This certainly is not a fair comment on the Nkrumah era. Granted that Nkrumah's regime committed certain fundamental mistakes in the course of steering the ship of state of Ghana, it is however to the eternal credit of the Nkrumah era that Ghana's independence was used to open the gates of liberation for many African Countries. Apart from these statements that are certainly ambiguous and unclear, the ideological character of the revolution still remains a mystery.

Many of the PNDC secretaries are Marxists and there is clear evidence of a growing socialist consciousness among the radical youths in Ghana as confirmed by Ato Austen in my interview with him, it is however doubtful whether Jerry Rawlings and many of his military colleagues in the PNDC share these revolutionary ideas. Jerry Rawlings has been quoted many times as stating that Ghana's revolution will not be fashioned on any particular ideology but will be guided by the genuine aspirations of the people. While an orthodox Marxist approach to solving the problems of Ghana will fail totally and increase the economic sufferings of the people it is however certain that a gradualist socialist approach will help the revolution in attaining its goals.

The problem of Ghana as I see it today is the presence of an ideologically committed followership but with an ambivalent and politically naive leadership. It is a total reversal of the trend in Nkrumah's Ghana where the leadership was ideological but the followership was naive and counter revolutionary. The CPP overseas group based in London has already warned Marxist forces to be careful of the Rawlings regime. The group that publishes the radical *Dawn* magazine is of the view that the Rawlings revolution in Ghana might generate into fascism. This may be an extreme position to take. From what I saw in Ghana, events may certainly push Jerry Rawlings into a clearer ideological position. He has moved several miles from his naive position of 1979 but has not been totally convinced of the need for a socialist struggle in Ghana.

The lack of ideological direction of the Revolution is certainly militating aginst the revolutionary zeal of the radical socialist forces who want to tackle Ghana's socio-economic problems purely on a socialist solution. Some of the methods being used by Rawlings now are surely cosmetic and unrealistic. If anything at all, the methods can erode the base of support for the regime. Some of these methods include incessant harassments of the market mammies over food prices and the rather unorthodox method of encouraging workers to take over their unions from those described as reactionary trade union leaders without any direction and guidance. I was in Accra when on 30th April 1980, the Ghana radio announced the occupation by several workers of the Ghana Trade Union secretariat. Officers described as counter revolutionary elements were said to have been removed. While the takeover of the TUC secretariat was said not to have had any state connections, I did not hesitate to tell my friends that the methods used by the radical workers who took over power in the trade union movement were basically fascist. Because the state had refused to spell out its ideological direction and way forward, thereby neutralising, with relative ease, forces who may want to obstruct the Revolution. I also said it was fascist for the workers to take laws into their hands without police support to eject their officers. I was sure the methods were clear "destroy the reactionary temple" attitude without an alternative plan to immediately build a progressive one. The TUC is now run by revolutionary forces who may never be able to say clearly the ideological road the revolution in Ghana is to take. The *West Africa* magazine based in London in its 12th May 1982 edition reported the take over of the TUC thus:

> Mr. E. K. Aboagye, interim chairman of the Association of Local Unions (ALU) has explained that the dismissal of the Trade Union Congress leadership from office by the ALU was a revolutionary necessity to guarantee the power to propel workers along the Revolution.
>
> The workers of Ghana, conscious of the leading role they have to play in the Revolution, would not allow bankrupt leadership and undemocratic institutions or structures to stand in the path of the revolution.

Addressing a workers' May Day rally in Accra, Mr. Aboagye reminded them that the Revolution had opened the way for the oppressed people to effectively seize power and steer national affairs on a path which would ensure the full and independent development of a democratic nation free from all forms of foreign control. "The Revolution has created the possiblity for an alliance of all revolutionary, progressive, democratic and patriotic people to unite to pull our nation out of its present state of advanced decay and degeneration," Mr. Aboagye emphasised.

These, no doubt, are beautiful words of a determined working class movement. The success of the forcible takeover of the TUC by revolutionary forces does not, however, end the whole drama. The dismissed trade union leaders have only been driven underground in view of what might have appeared to them a move supported by the PNDC. These leaders may rear their heads up again to give a fight if reaction ever attempts to fight back and the threat of this is real in Ghana.

Revolutions are festivals of the oppressed. Total mobilisation is achieved in every state gripped with revolutionary fervour. This can not be said of events in Ghana. Jerry Rawlings is no doubt a very popular leader. His elegance, charm, sincerity of purpose and anti corruption crusade have won him the respect and admiration of millions of people in Ghana. All these however do not make for the type of mobilisation that one would like to see in a country that has proclaimed a revolution. The only mobilised section of the Ghana society today is the student's movement. The student's movement may, however, not be a permanent and reliable ally of the revolution in view of the fact that the majority of African students are still the very epitome of our continent's cultural identity crisis.

The crowds gather in their thousands only when Rawlings is to speak. No more no less. On May Day, the international day of solidarity of the working class movement, I was surprised to find that not many workers were at the May Day rally held at the Black Star Square in Accra. The workers who came for the rally were few and I did not waste time in telling some comrades who were with me that the scene was not a good representation of the Revolution that is said to be on in Ghana. I warned them (and I am still warning) of the danger of not allowing the messages of the Revolution to be grasped by the masses of the people. The tone and music of the Revolution must be raised all the time so as to fire and awaken the enthusiasm of the masses of the people.

A part of the cosmetism of the methods being used to forge the Ghana revolution ahead is the renaming of the Ghana Army as the People's Army. A people's army connotes an army based on socialist ideological principles. This is however far from being the case in Ghana. A people's army is an army of workers and peasants completely dedicated to fighting all anti revolutionary forces and influence in society and defending the rights and privileges of a socialist revolutionary regime. The establishment of a people's army is a total acceptance of the failure of the traditional army based on imperialist training and orientation. It also involves a total democratisation of the military establishment. Jerry Rawlings may be striving to achieve this now but this was far from being the case when I visited Ghana in April 1982.

11
The Ghana Revolution Must Succeed

It will be a tragedy of unequal proportions if the Ghana Revoution fails. The African Revolution may itself suffer a big setback as a result. This is why all African patriots must support the Revolution to succeed.

Imperialism will never wish Ghana under Jerry Rawlings well. Imperialism will never want to see Ghana embrace a revolutionary ideological stance the completely neutralises its position in the country. Rawlings and his youthful supporters spent the first few weeks of the Revolution demonstrating against imperialist moves to subvert their patriotic moves. The American Embassy that had been the scene of major demonstrations by the workers and students did not waste much time in errecting a giant barbed wire fence to ward off any violent demonstration. It was also a sign that America was quite prepared to fight back. The wait and see attitude of imperialism over the Ghana Revolution is no doubt a potential threat to the Revolution.

The CAMPAIGN FOR DEMOCRACY movement was launched in London by remnants of Hilla Limann's PNP. The group is led by Mr Justice Hayfron Benjamin. Lies are being manufactured to paint the Revolution dangerous. Ghana's former Ambassador to Nigeria, Alhaji Youssif Patty, at a world press conference in Lagos, lied that 2,750 Ghanaians had been killed during the coup with some 800 people wounded. It was a deliberate lie told to whip up international reaction against the Ghana Revolution. This is a clear game played by imperialism and its lackeys when planning their counter-revolutionary insurgencies.

A good socialist and nationalist to imperialism is a dead one. Allende of Chile was pursued until he was killed right in the Moneda Palace in 1973 by world imperialist forces. His offence was that he had committed Chile to the socialist road. There have been repressions of socialist forces in Sudan, Egypt and Zaire. On 7th November 1975 in faraway Bangladesh, a young army officer, Colonel Abu Taher (a Marxist-oriented army officer) staged a counter coup to effect the release of General Zia-Ul Rahman who, at the time was the Chief of Staff, of the Bangladesh army. A coup had earlier taken place in the country led by Brigadier Musharaf and the coup had succeeded in arresting Major Genral Zia-Ul-Rahman. Colonel Abu Taher, imbued with fervent patriotism, moved to town within seventy-two hours of Musharaf's coup and installed Major General Rahman as the new Head of State of the Republic of Bangladesh. Major General Zia-Ul Rahman was to later turn against Colonel Abu Taher and his colleagues who had staged the coup. He arrested all of them and had them tried for treason. On 21st July 1976, Colonel Abu Taher was hanged in Dacca Central prison, Bangladesh. A wave of massive repression of the left followed on the orders of Rahman. On Saturday 29th May 1981, the red-eyed dictator, Major General Zia-Ul-Rahman paid the price of treachery when he was shot dead in a bizarre manner by one of his trusted military colleagues at Chittagong town in Bangladesh.

Revolutionary forces are never spared by reactionary forces. So it was with Colonel Utung's left wing attempted coup in Indonesia in October 1965. The right wing forces immediately pulled together and under the leadership of General Suharto suppressed Utung's coup, dismissed the Sukarno regime and repressed the left in the country. It was a terrible purge of the left quite unprecendented in history.

It will be quite sad if thé Ghana Revolution eventually ends up consuming its own children. Rawlings must decide what path he will want the Ghana revoltion to take.

The Ghana Revolution must succeed. If the Revolution fails, the tragedy attendant to it will be too dreadful to recount. The Revolution offers great hopes for a better tomorrow for the masses of the African people. Jerry Rawlings must ensure that green leaves are not destroyed while the dry ones are still standing erect in Ghana.

The struggle definitely continues.

INDEX

Aboagye, E. K.	99
Accra Evening News	3
Acheampong, Col. (later Gen.) Ignatius Kutu	7, 11-12, 15-21, 23-5, 39, 47
ideologies and policies	19
Union Government proposals	26-38, 42-3, 43-4, 83
overthrow of	39-43
Adamafio, Tawia	52
Addae-Mensah, Dr. Ivan	69
Aferi, Major-Gen. Emmanuel	14-15
African Youth Command	19, 26
Afrifa, Gen. Akwasi Amankwaa	12, 14, 47, 52
Agbo, Major Kodzo B.	15, 24
Aidoo, Ama Atta, interview with	83-6
Akatapore, Sgt Alolga	76
Akuffo, Gen. Fred	40, 43-5, 47, 53, 57
Angola	2
Ankrah, Gen. Joseph A.	4, 12, 14
Armed Forces Revolutionary Council (AFRC)	5, 7, 8, 48, 55
Association of Recognised Professional Bodies	27, 32-4
Austin, Ato	94
interview with	86-91, 94
Awolowo, Chief Obafemi	19, 71, 76-7
Awoonor, Dr. Kofi	24
Ayarna, Alhaji Imoru	24
Baah, Major Kwame	15, 24
Batsa, Kofi	69
Beausoleil, Major-Gen.	25
Bekoe, Nana Okutwer	54, 68-9
Ben Barka, Mohammed	17
Bernasko, Col. Frank	17
Boakye-Gyan, Major	8, 55, 59
Boakyi, Air Vice-Marshall G. Y.	41, 47
Botsio, Kojo	24, 52
Busia, Dr. Kofi Abrefa	5-7, 11-16, 83
Charter of Redemption	18
Chiavelli, Marino	70
Convention People's Party (CPP)	6, 13-14, 20, 52-3, 98
coups:	
24 Feb 1966	1, 2, 4
17 April 1967 (attempted)	12-13
13 June 1972	7, 11-12, 15-16
4 June 1979	7, 13, 46-7; 31
31 December 1981	5, 14, 73-80, 93

Index

Da Rocha, Moses Ambrose	24-5
Daniels, Prof. Ekow	71
De Graft Johnson, Dr.	70
Egala, Alhaji Imoru	48, 53, 54, 68
Felli, Col. Roger	47
Gaddafi, Muammar	59
Ghana Bar Association	26, 43
Ghana Peace and Solidarity Council	19, 26
Ghana Trade Union Congress	6, 7, 98-100
Gyawu-Kyem, Kwame	28-31
Hansen, John	6, 53, 55
interview with,	81-3
Harley, John	12
Houphouet-Boigny, Felix	15, 16-17
imperialism	2-5, 12-17
Kattah, Brig. A. K.	24
Keita, Modibo	17
Kerekou, Mathieu	59
Kissinger, Henry	20, 30
Kotei, Gen. Robert	24, 41-2, 47
Kotoka, Col. Emmanuel	12, 52
Legon Observer	13-14
Limann, Hilla	48-50, 53-7, 59-60, 65
government of	67-71, 73-4, 76
Mao Tse-Tung	7-8, 20, 29
Marxism	3, 6
Mozambique	2
Nasser, Abdel Gamal	17
National Liberation Council (NLC)	4, 5, 12-14
National Redemption Council (NRC)	39
National Union of Ghana Students (NUGS)	5, 20, 27, 28-31
neo-colonialism	4, 5
Kkrumah, Kwame	1-5, 6, 8, 12, 14, 16, 17, 18, 20, 51, 52, 54, 82, 90
Class Struggle in Africa	1
Africa must unite	3-4
Nkrumaism	1-6, 8, 9, 12, 14, 16-18, 20, 51-2, 54, 82, 90
pan-Africanism	5, 15
People's Front Party (PFP)	69
People's National Party (PNP)	8, 18, 37, 48, 53-5, 67-8, 86-7, 95
People's Popular Party	6
Poku-Mensah, Major	8, 55, 59

Provisional National Defence Council (PNDC)	6, 84, 97-8, 100
Rawlings, John Jerry	1, 4,.7, 8, 13, 14, 24, 37, 44-5, 46-9, 54-5, 57-60, 65, 74-5, 82-3, 89-90, 93, 95-8, 100
Sekou Touré,	17
Selormey, Col. Anthony	15, 24
Senghor, Leopold Sedar	17
Shagari, Alhaji Shehu	71
socialism	2-4
South Africa	5, 15-16
Spark	3
Supreme Military Council	24, 32-5, 41-2, 44
Tettegah, John	24, 52, 54-5
Tolbert, Dr. William	15
Utuka, Gen. E. K.	42, 47
Vorster, Balthasar	5
Wellington, Gen. Odartey	23, 45, 46
Winneba Ideological Institute	2
Zimbabwe	2

www.ingramcontent.com/pod-product-compliance
Lightning Source LLC
Chambersburg PA
CBHW021410290426
44108CB00010B/468